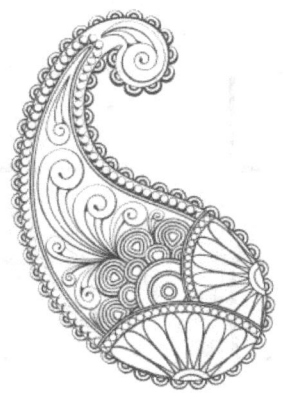

This Henna Style Coloring Book belongs to:

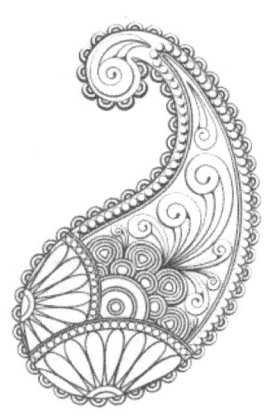

_____

_____

Color Test

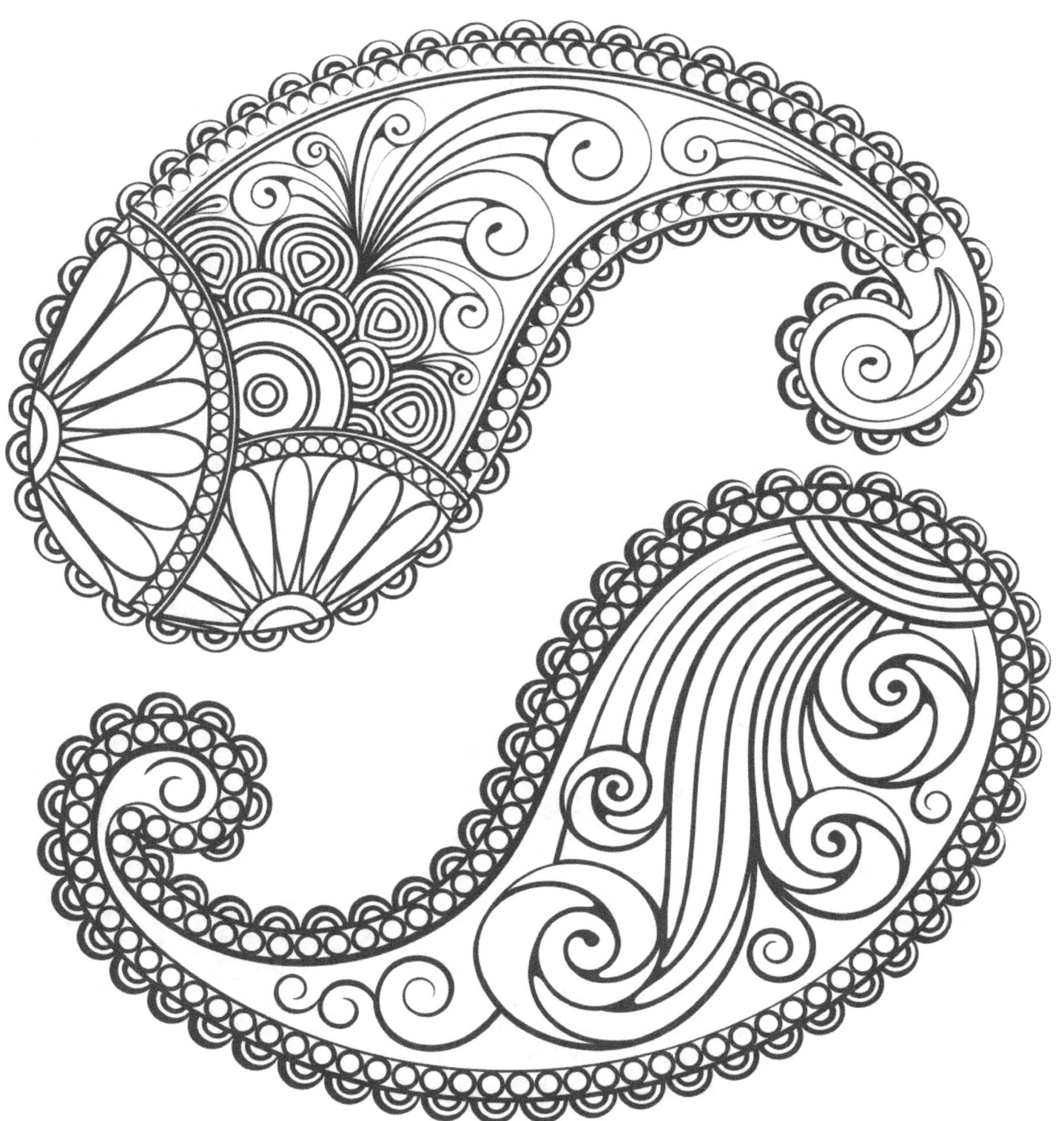

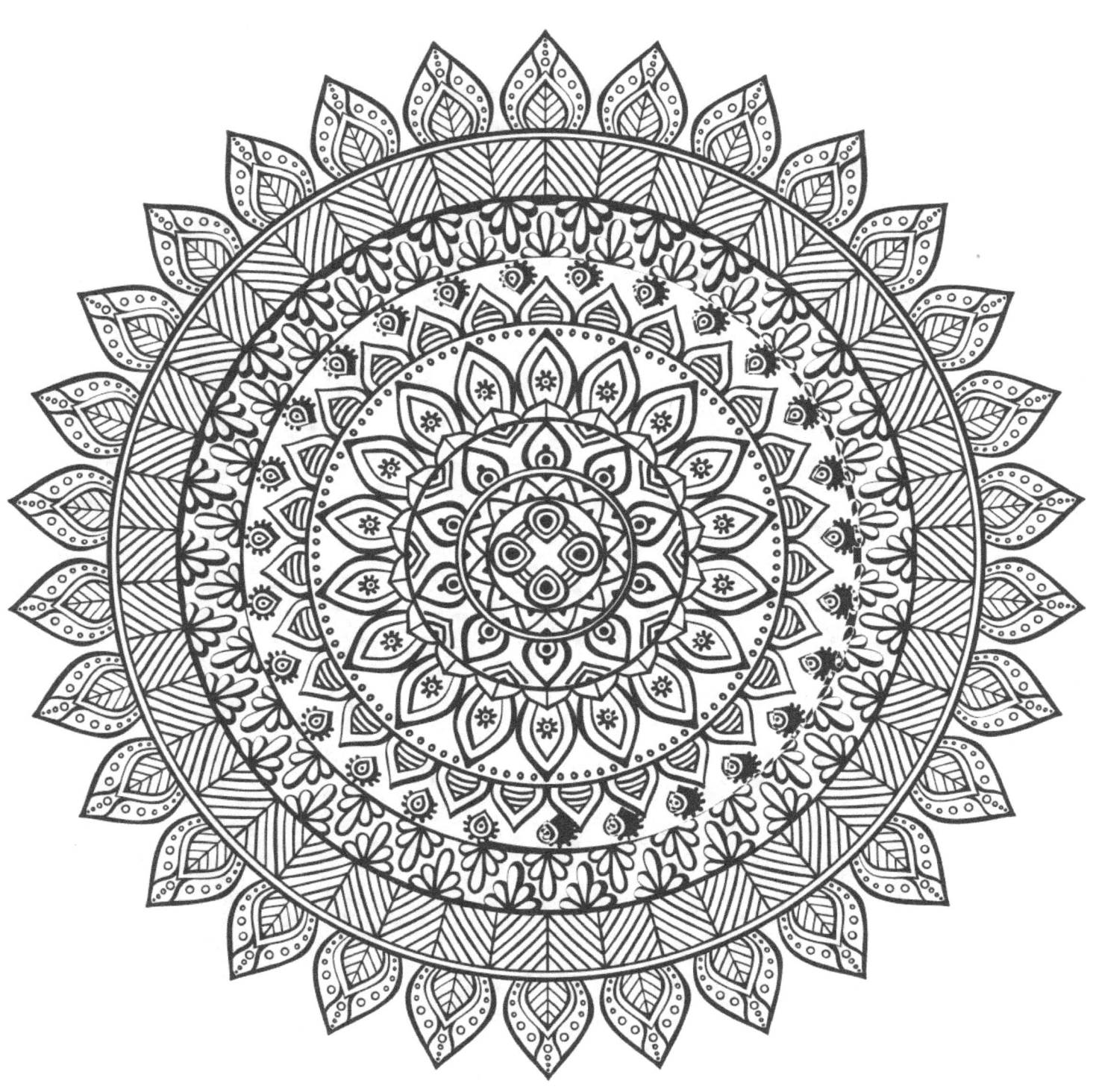

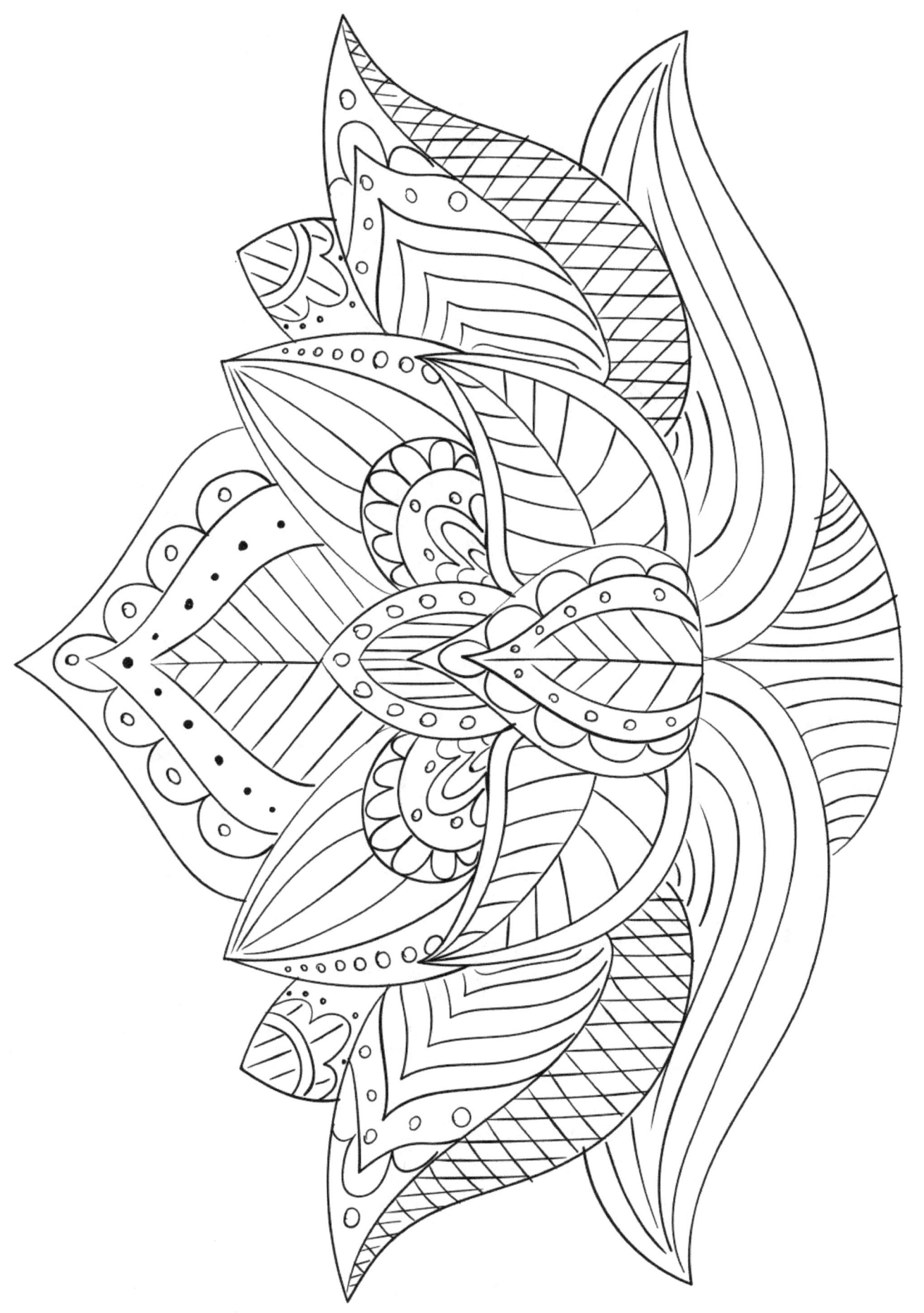

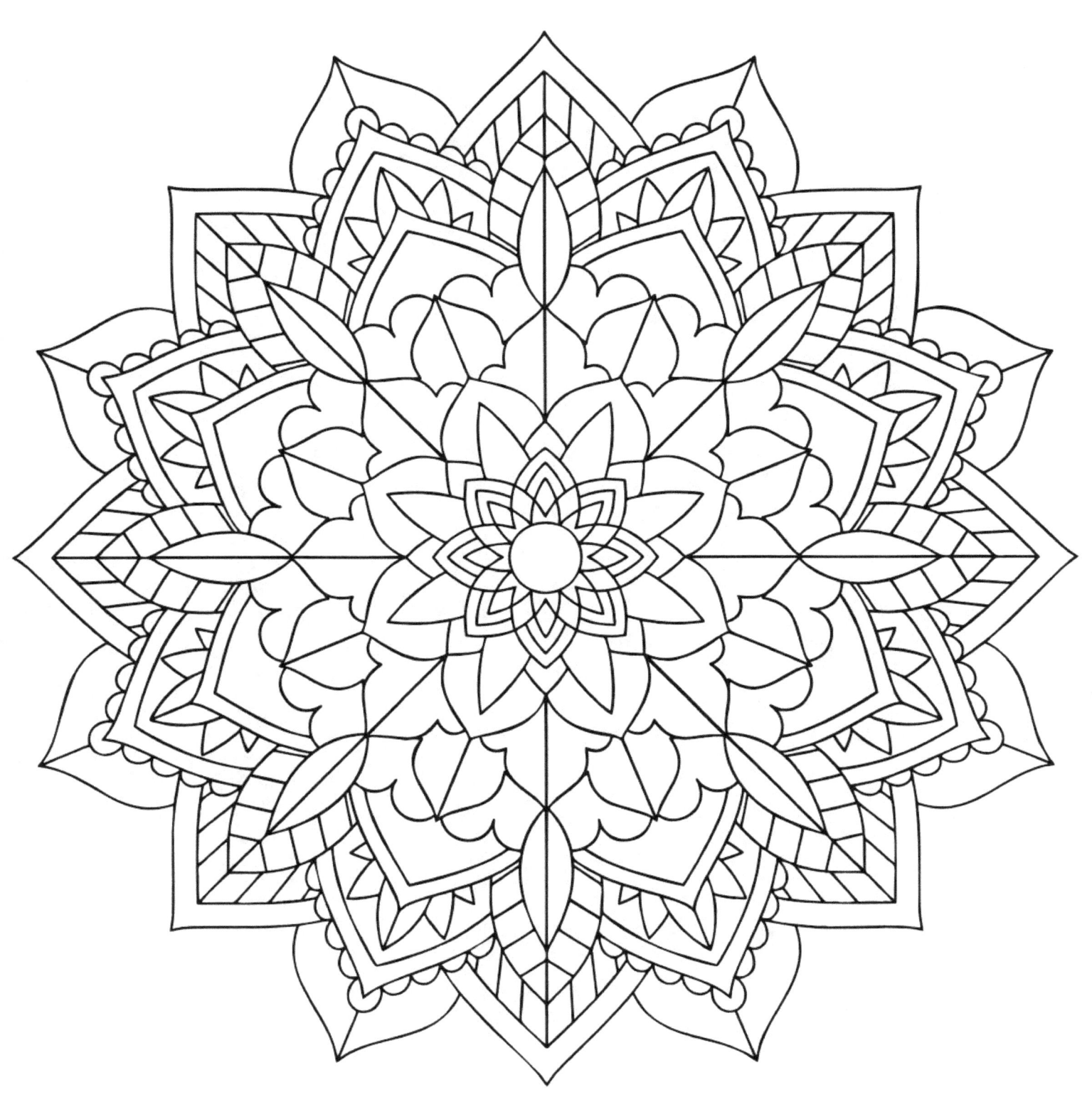

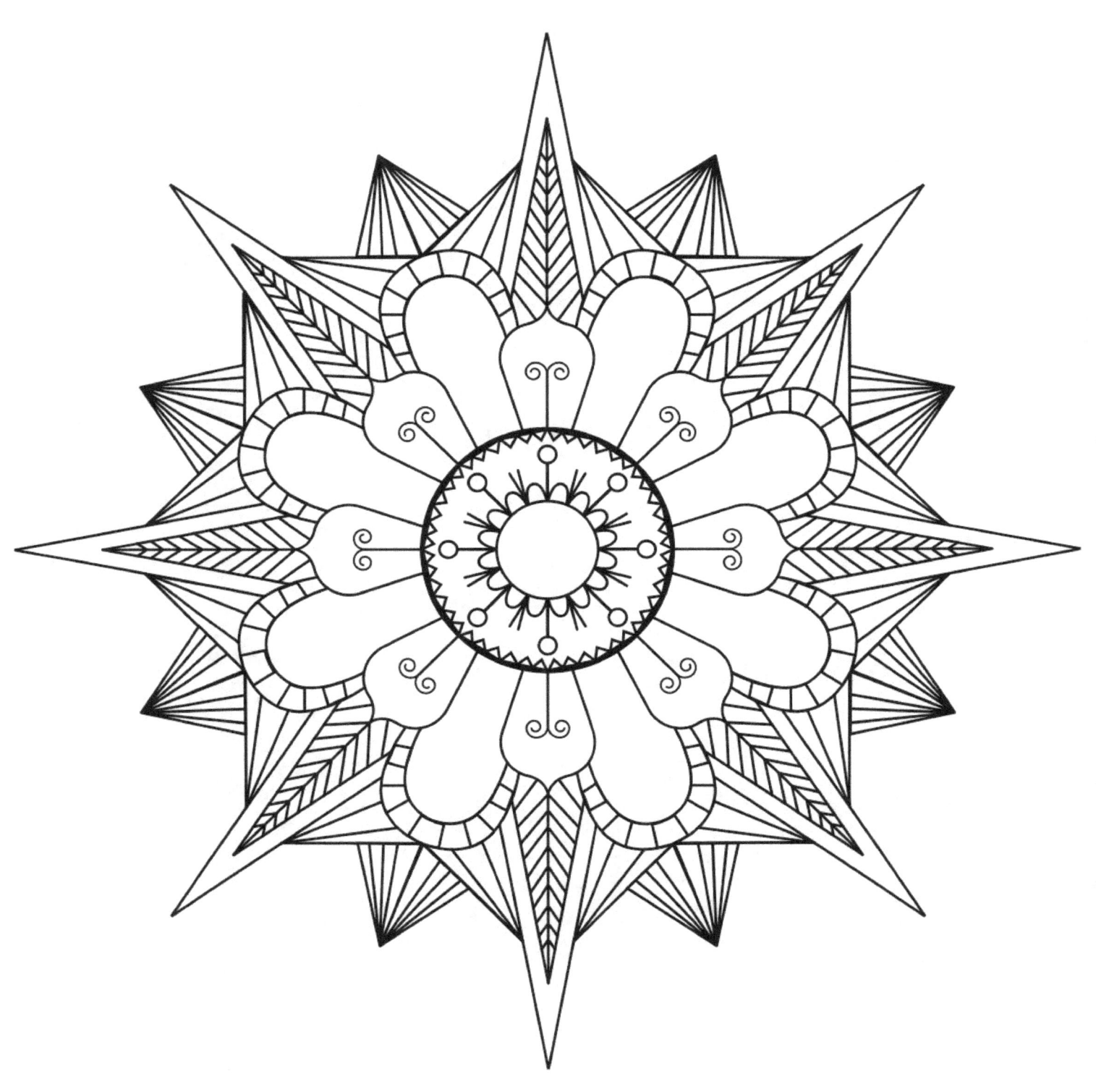

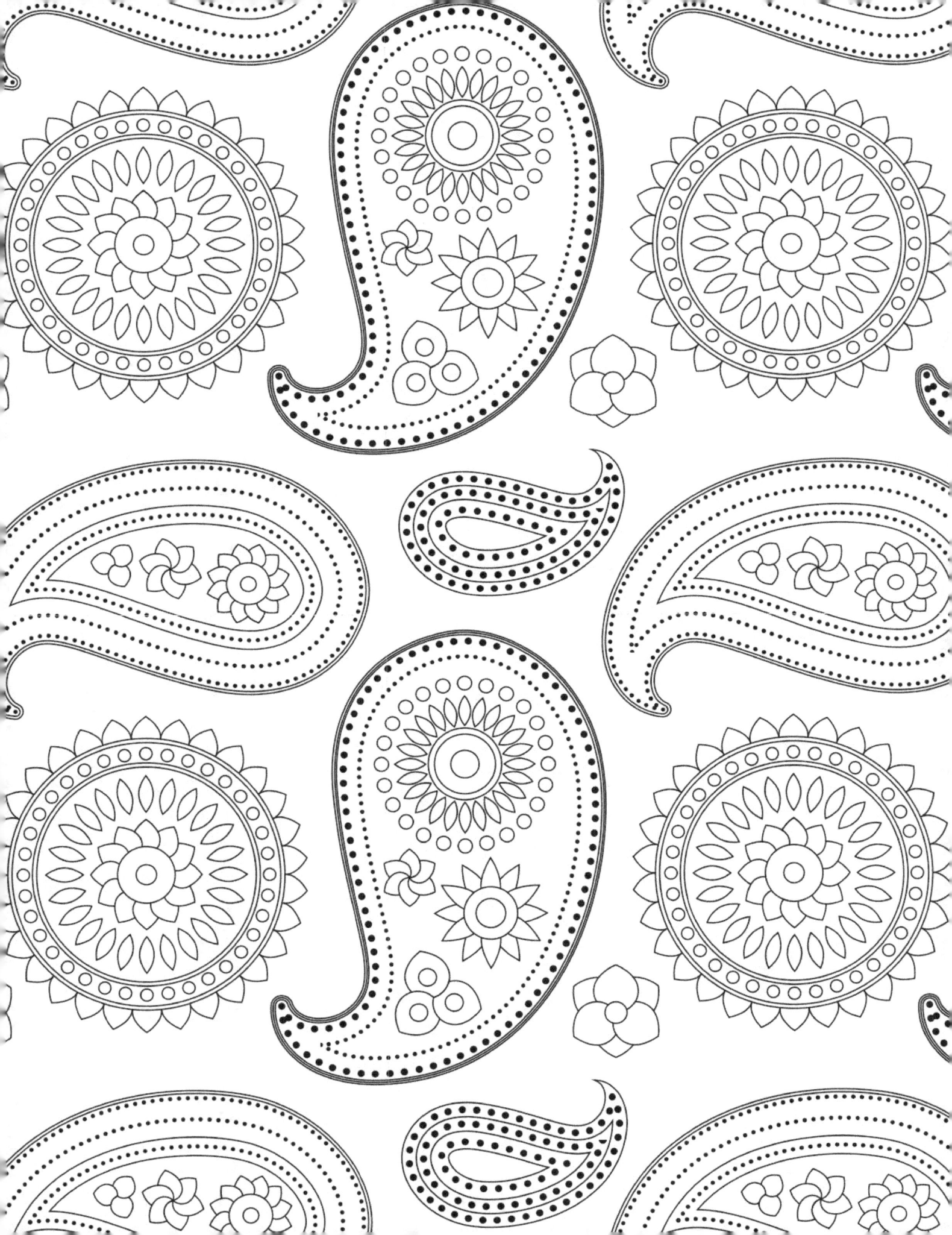

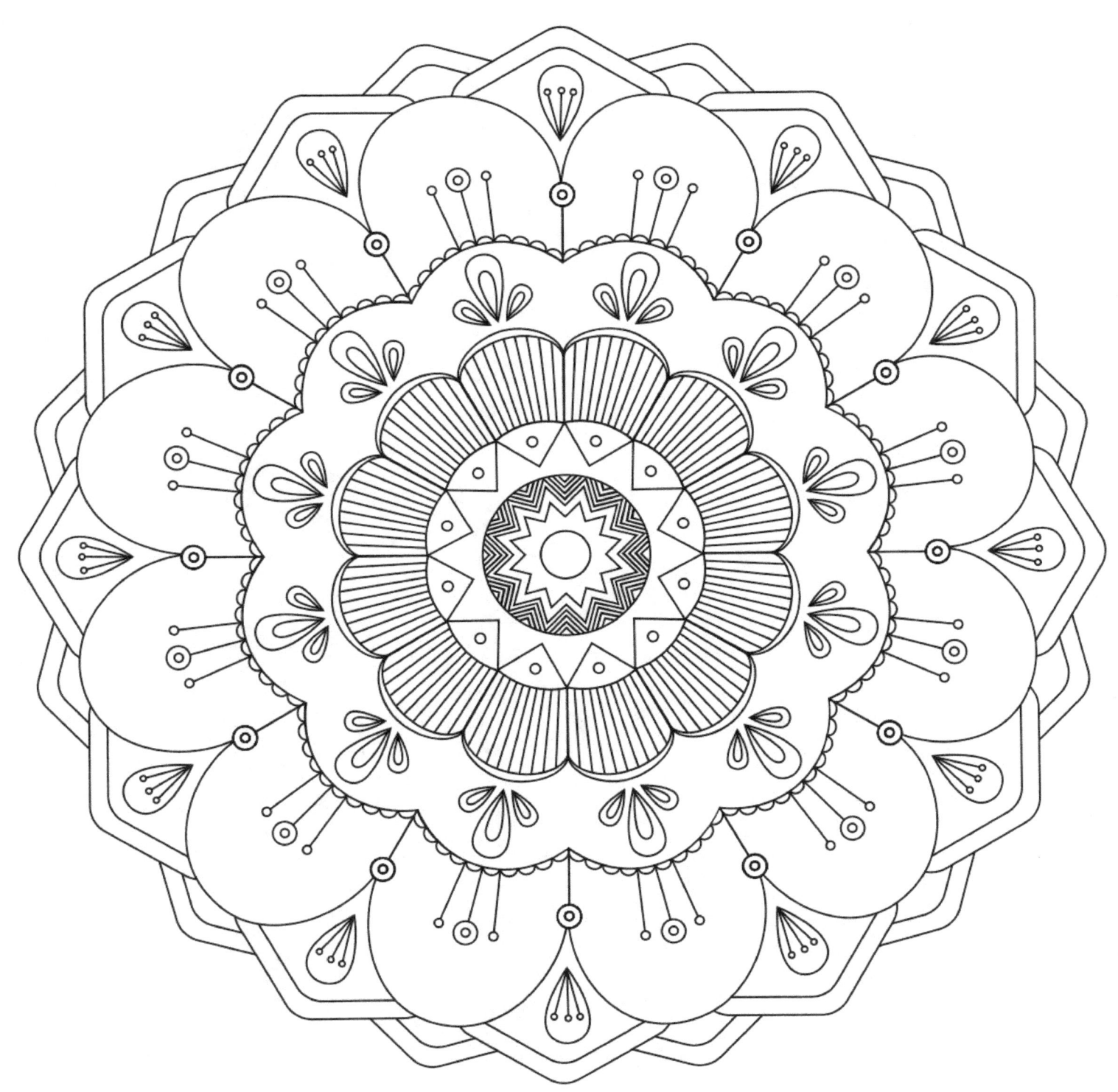

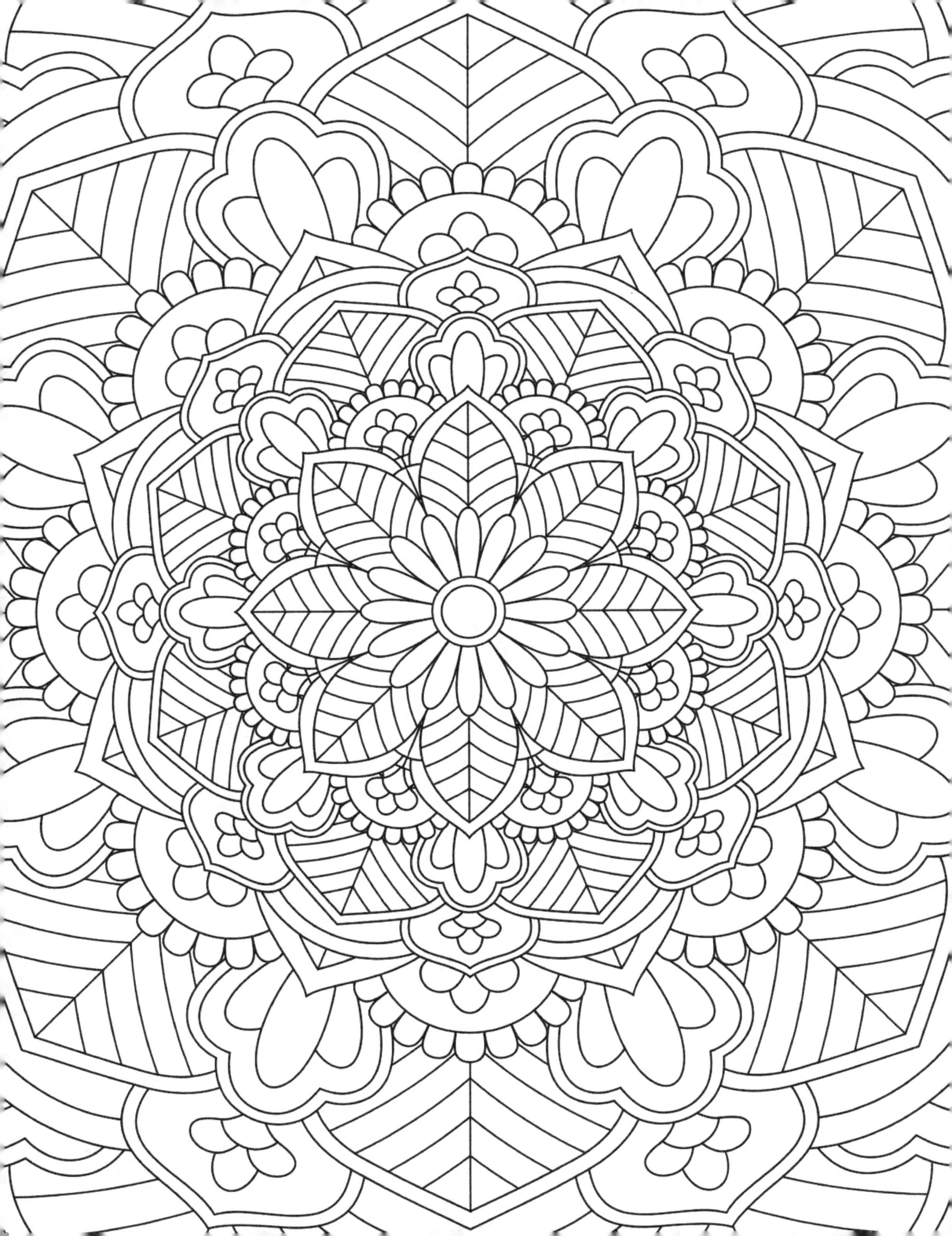

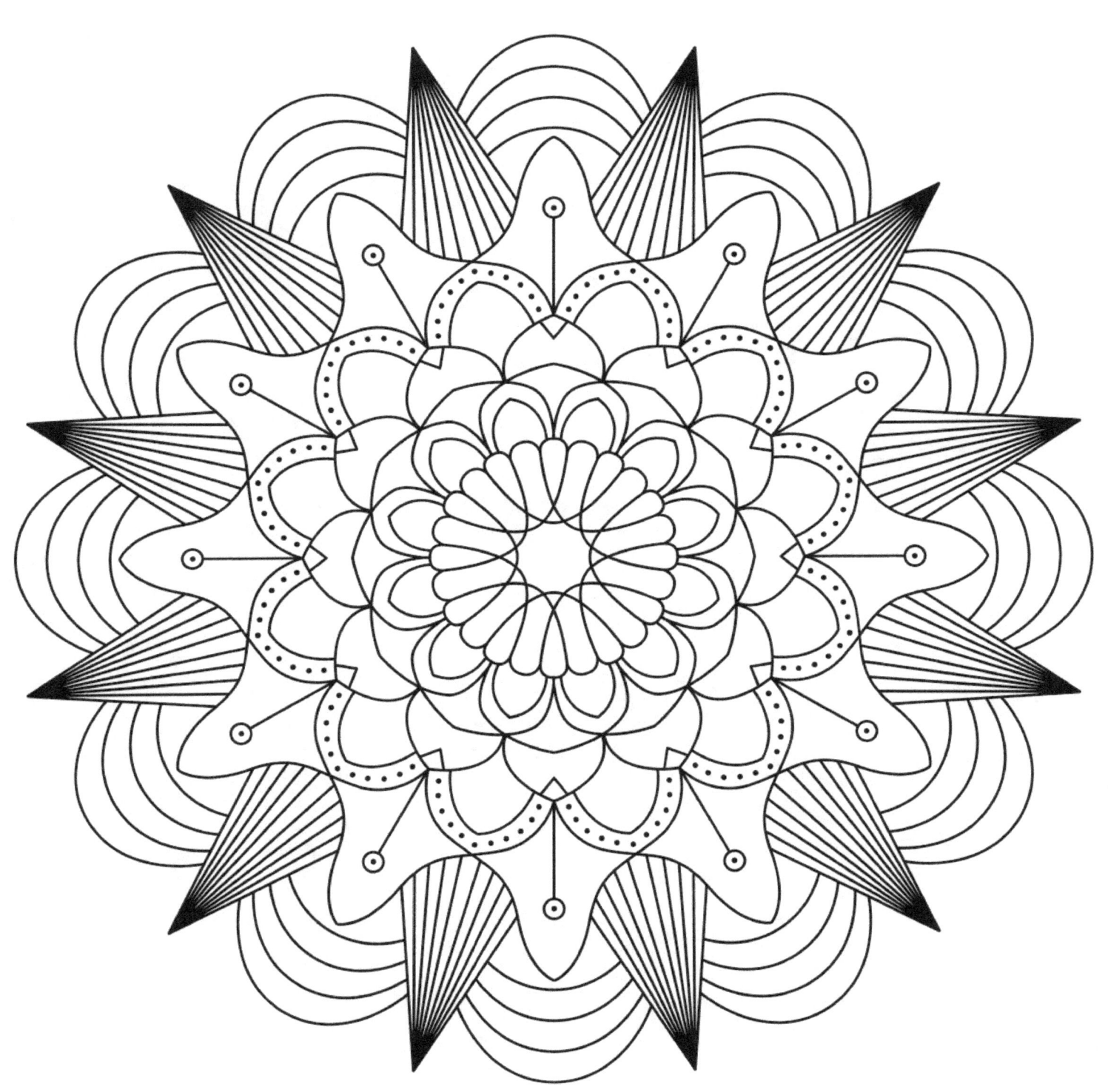

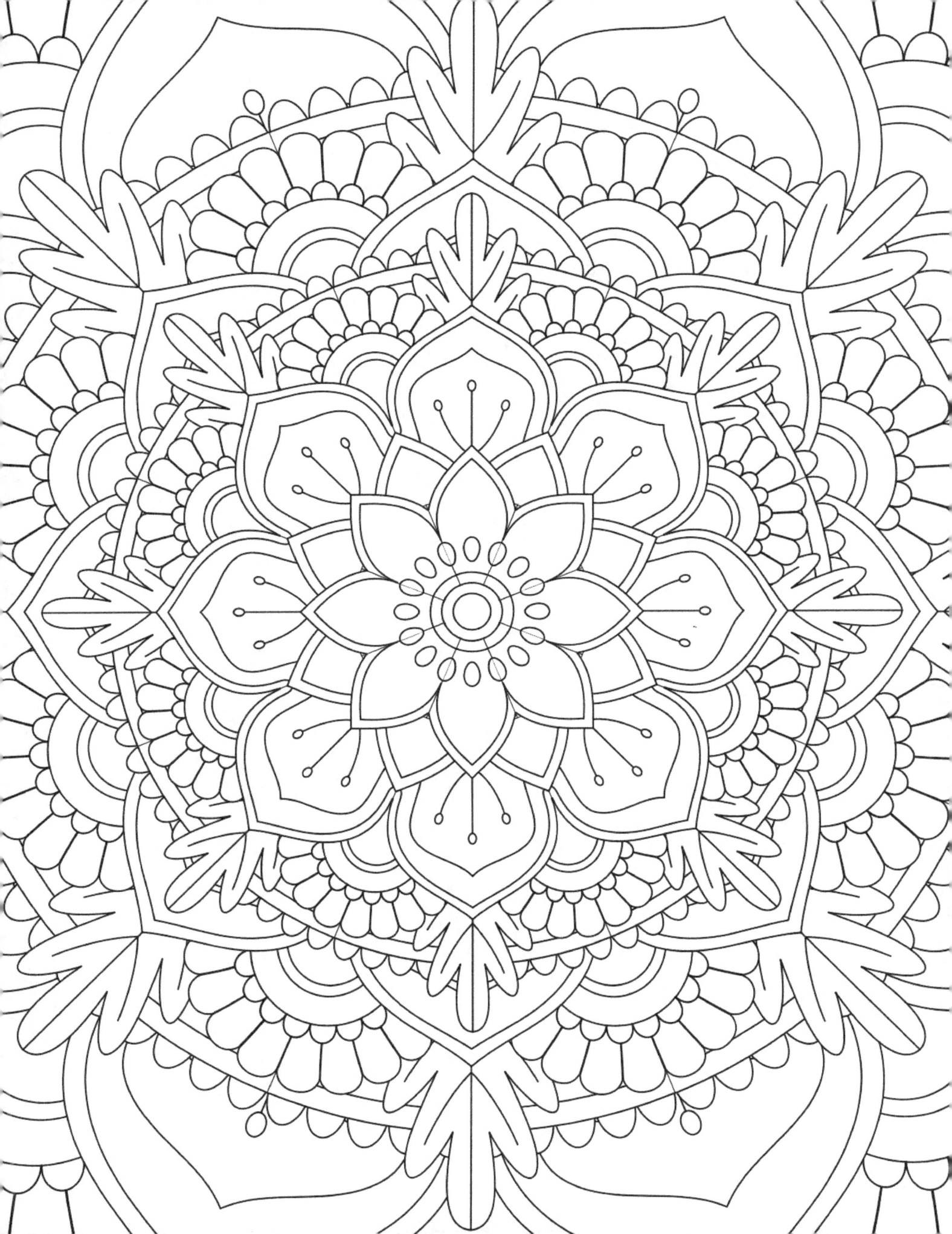

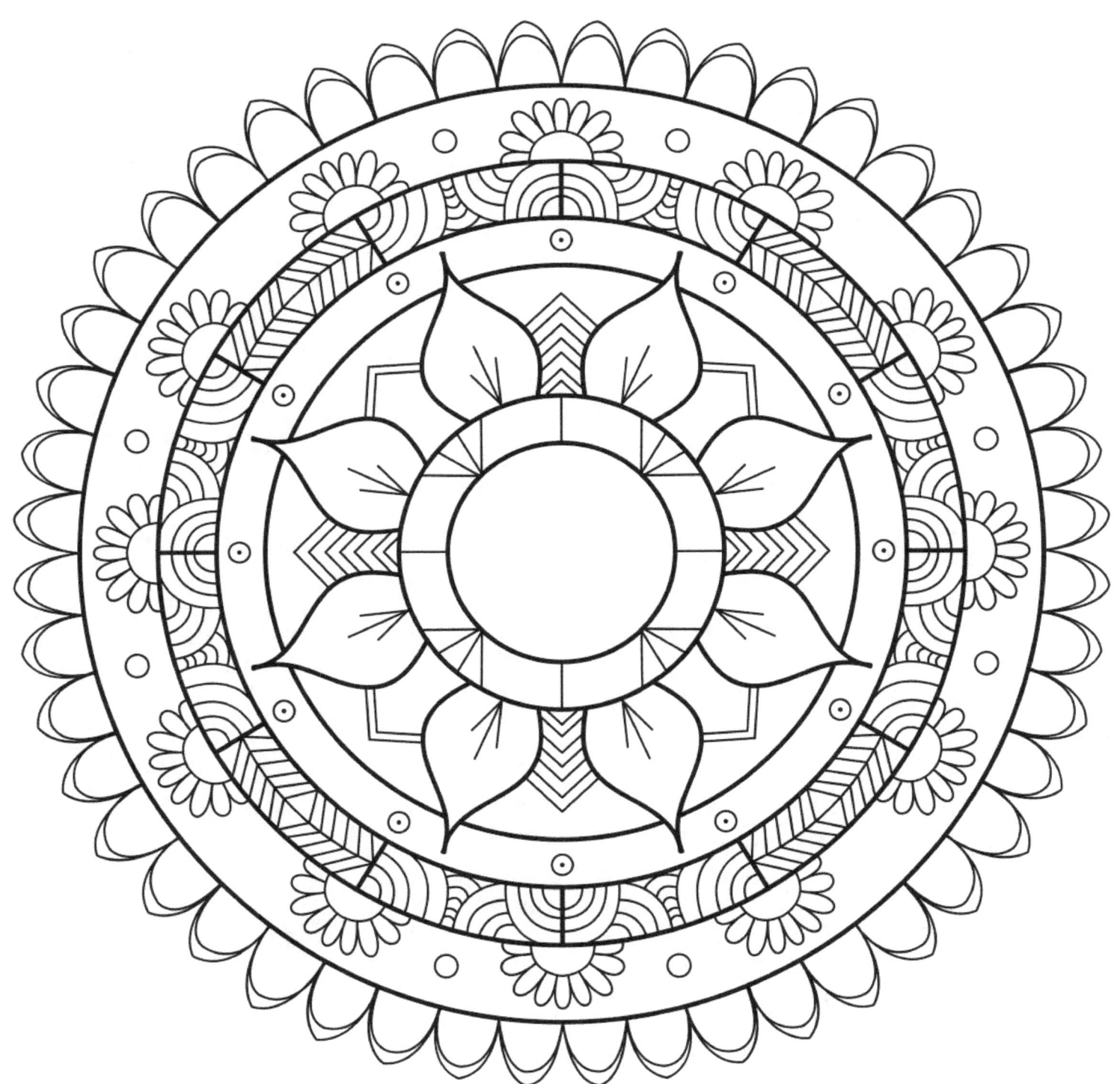

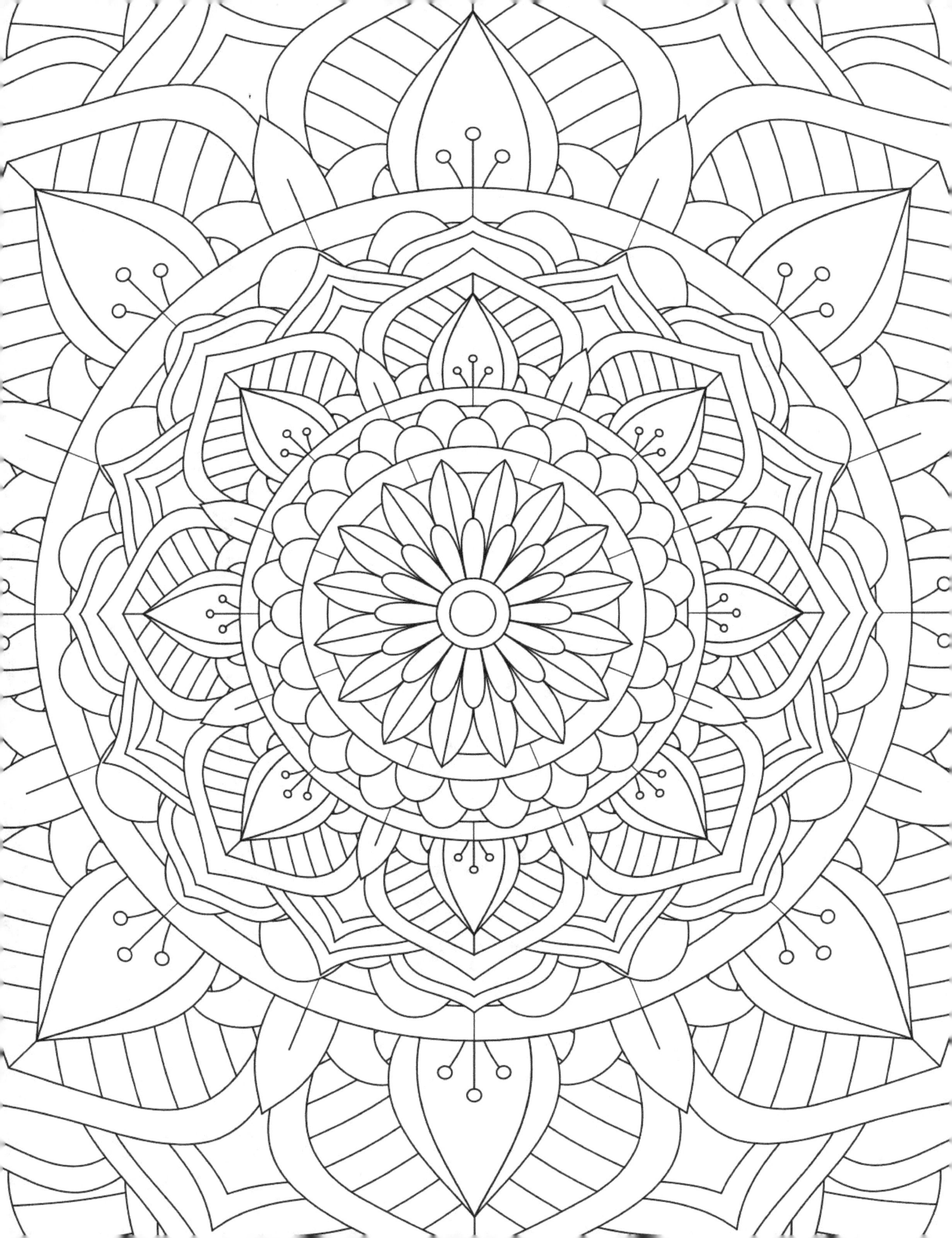

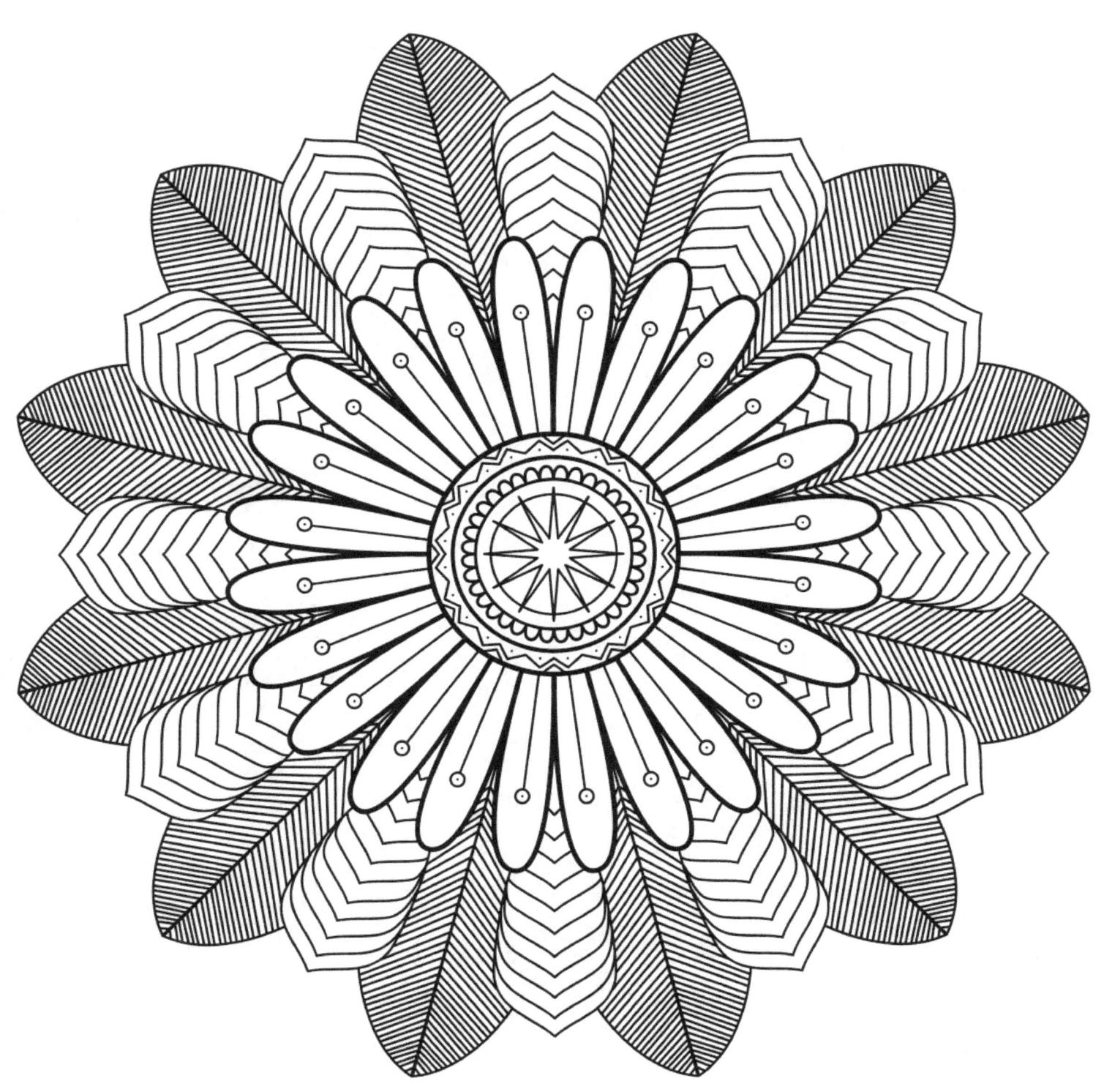

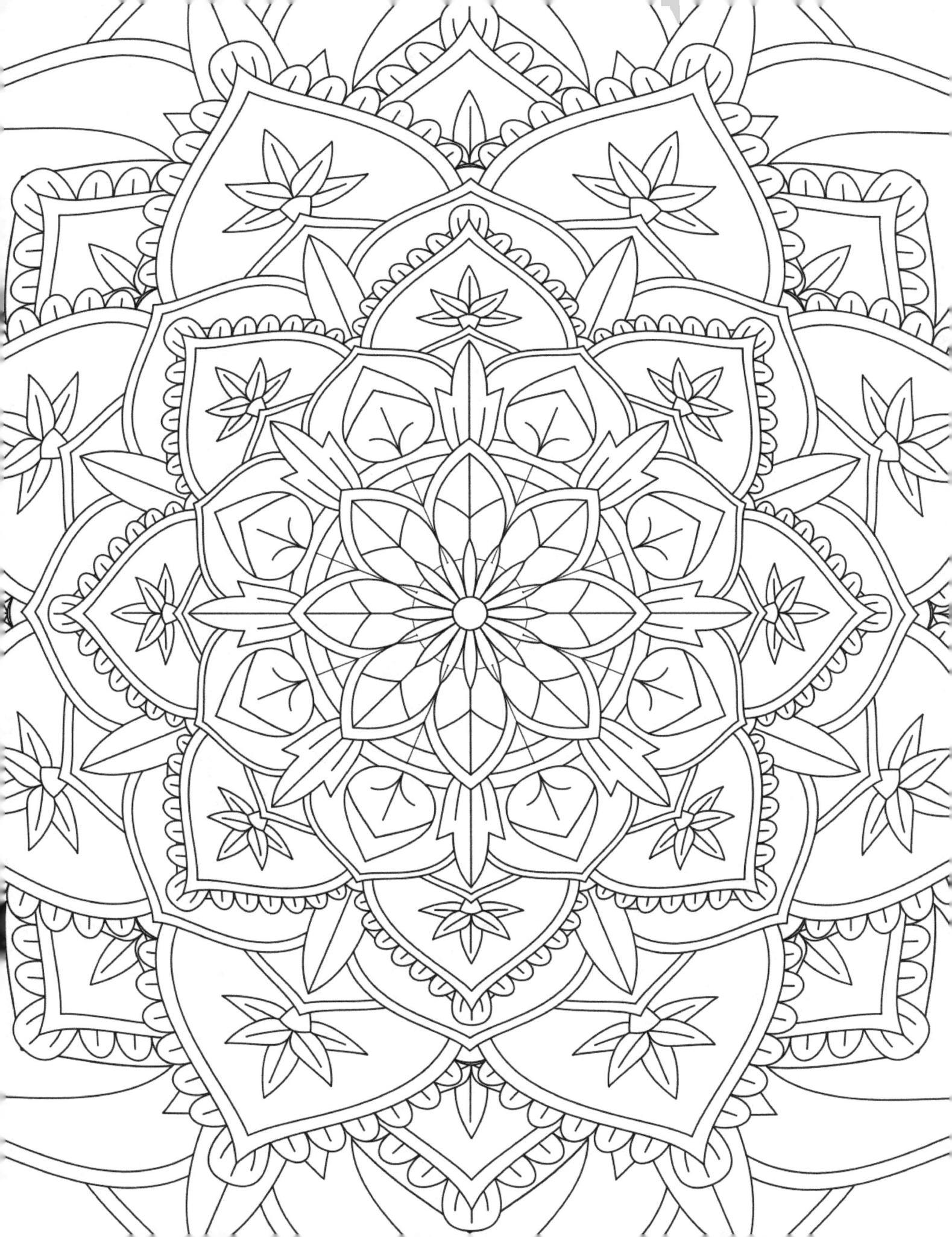

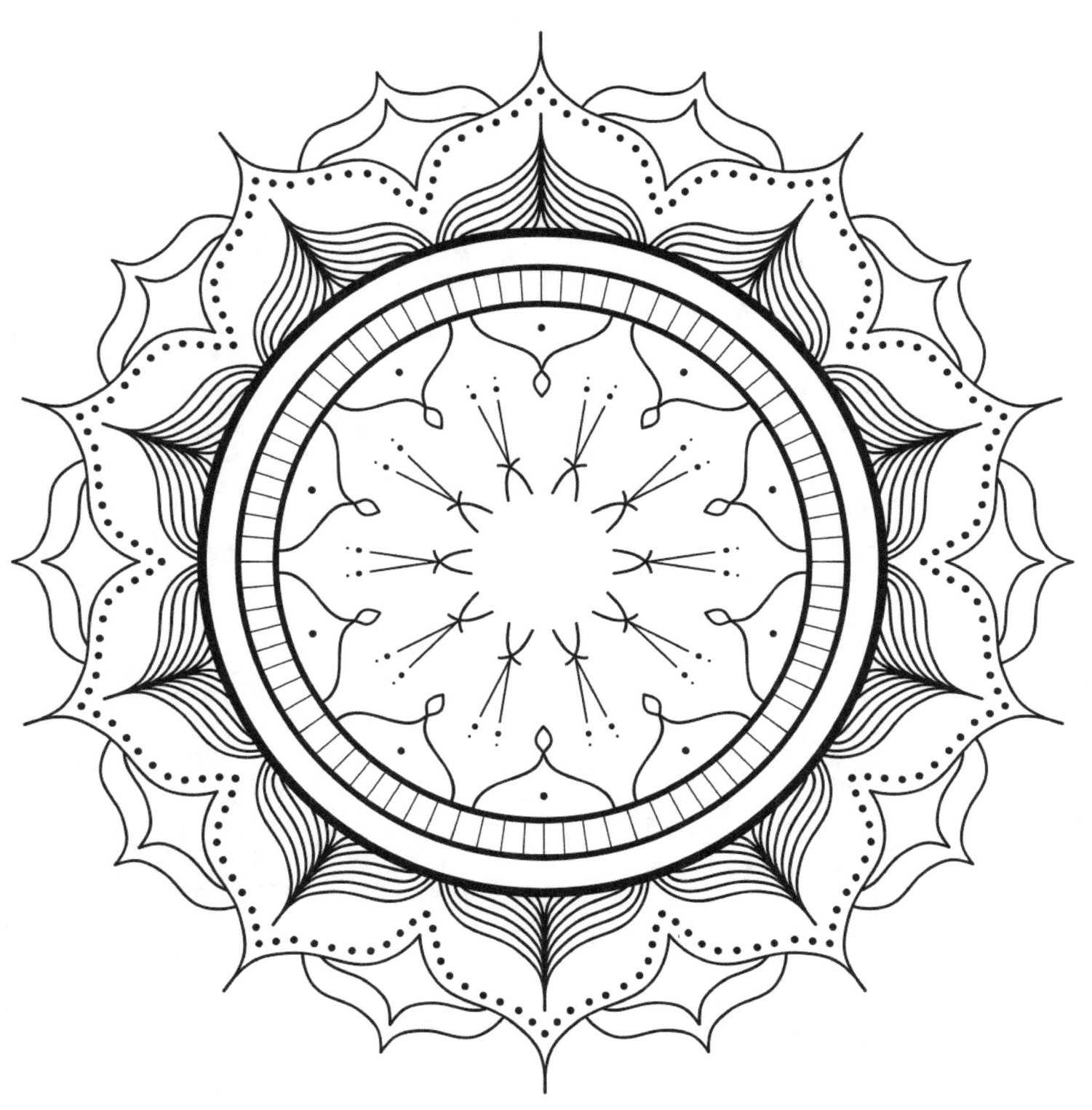

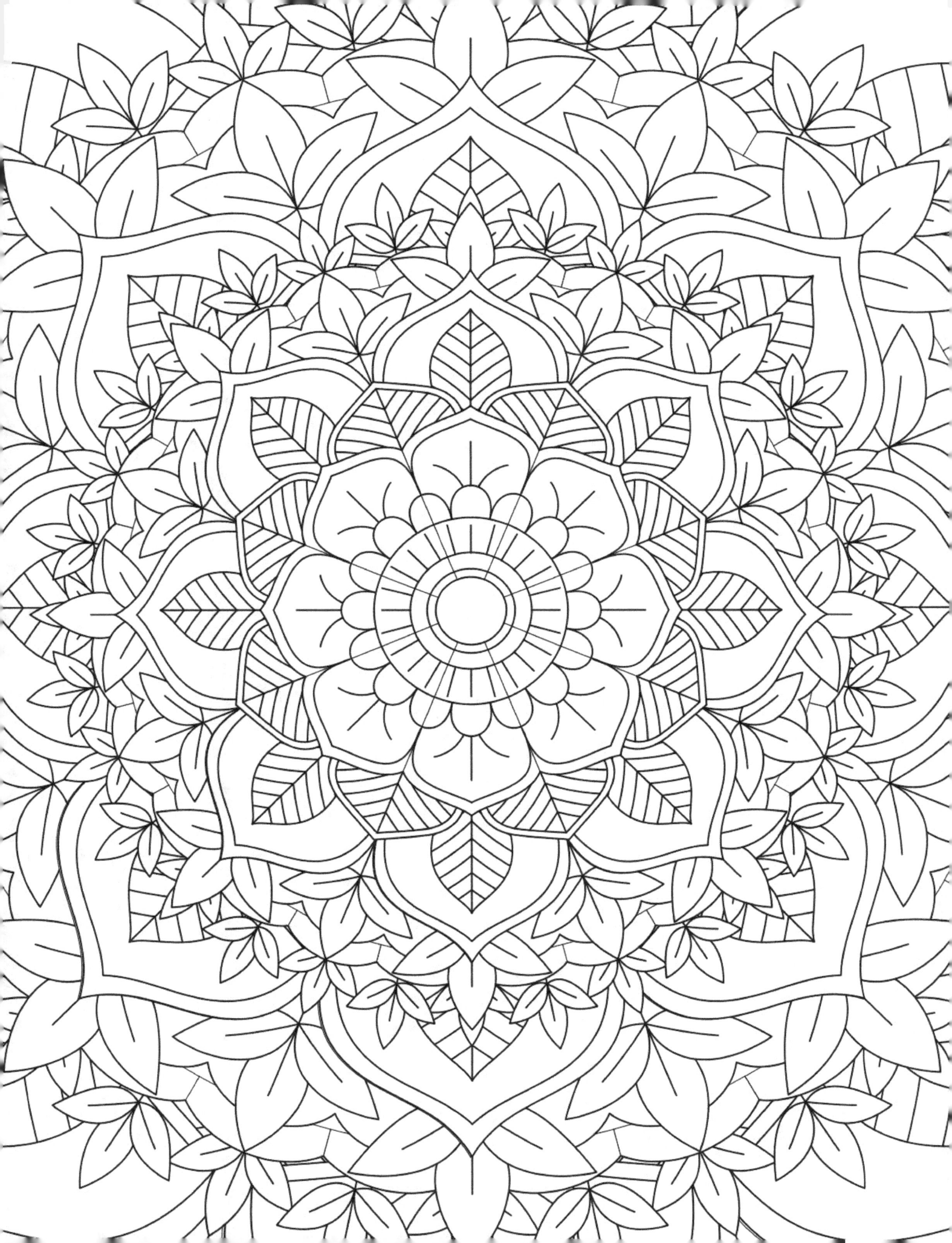

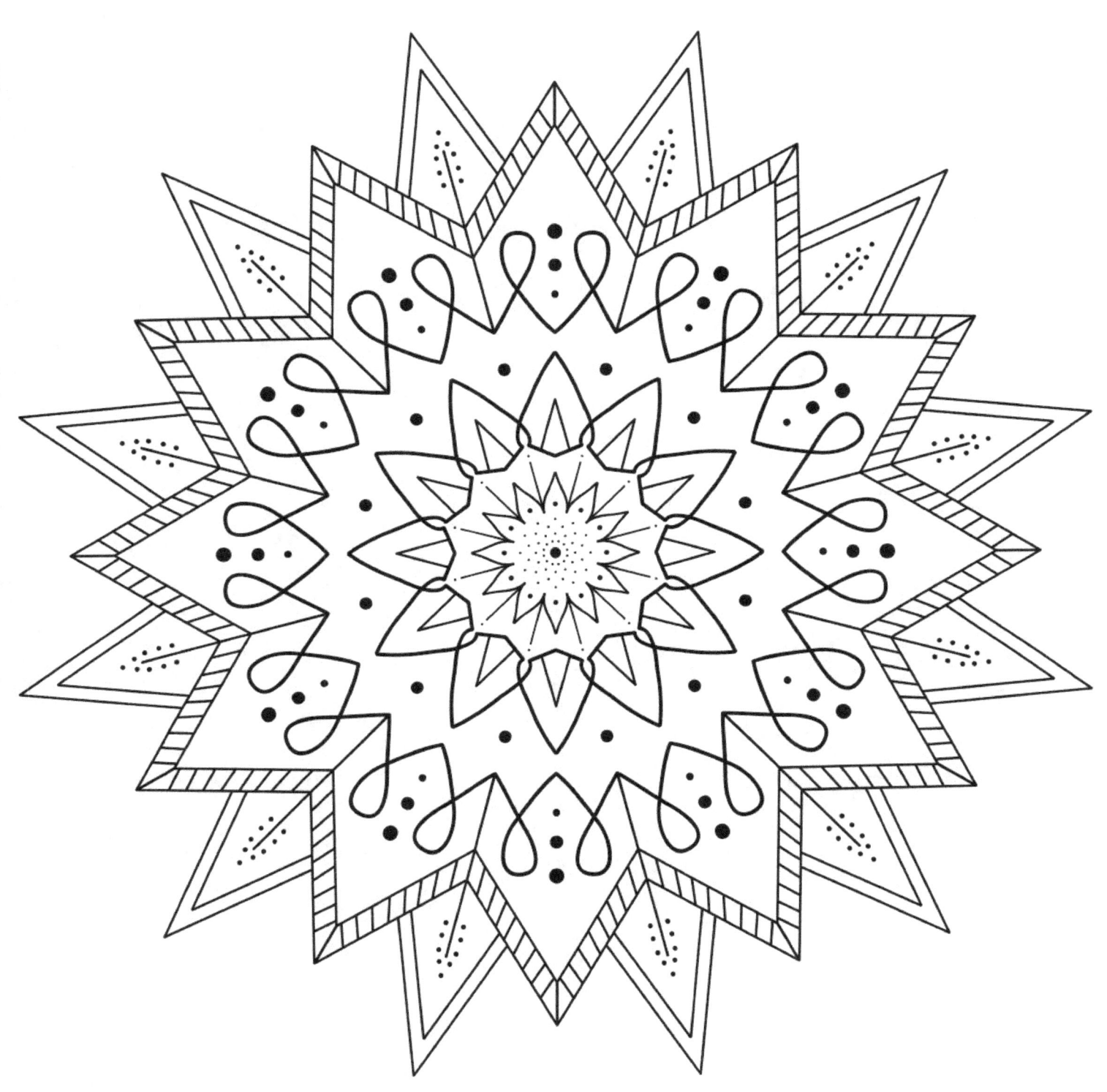

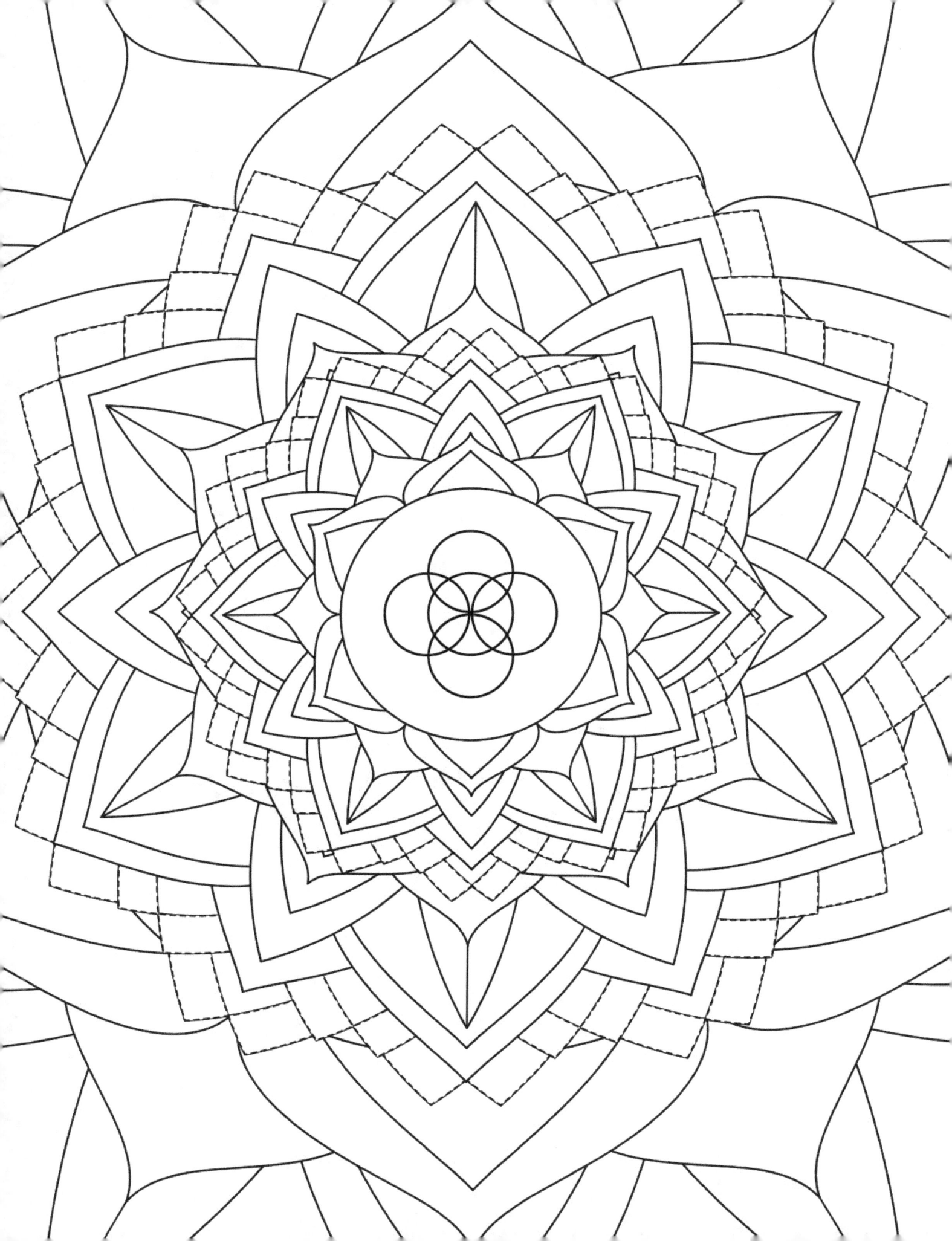

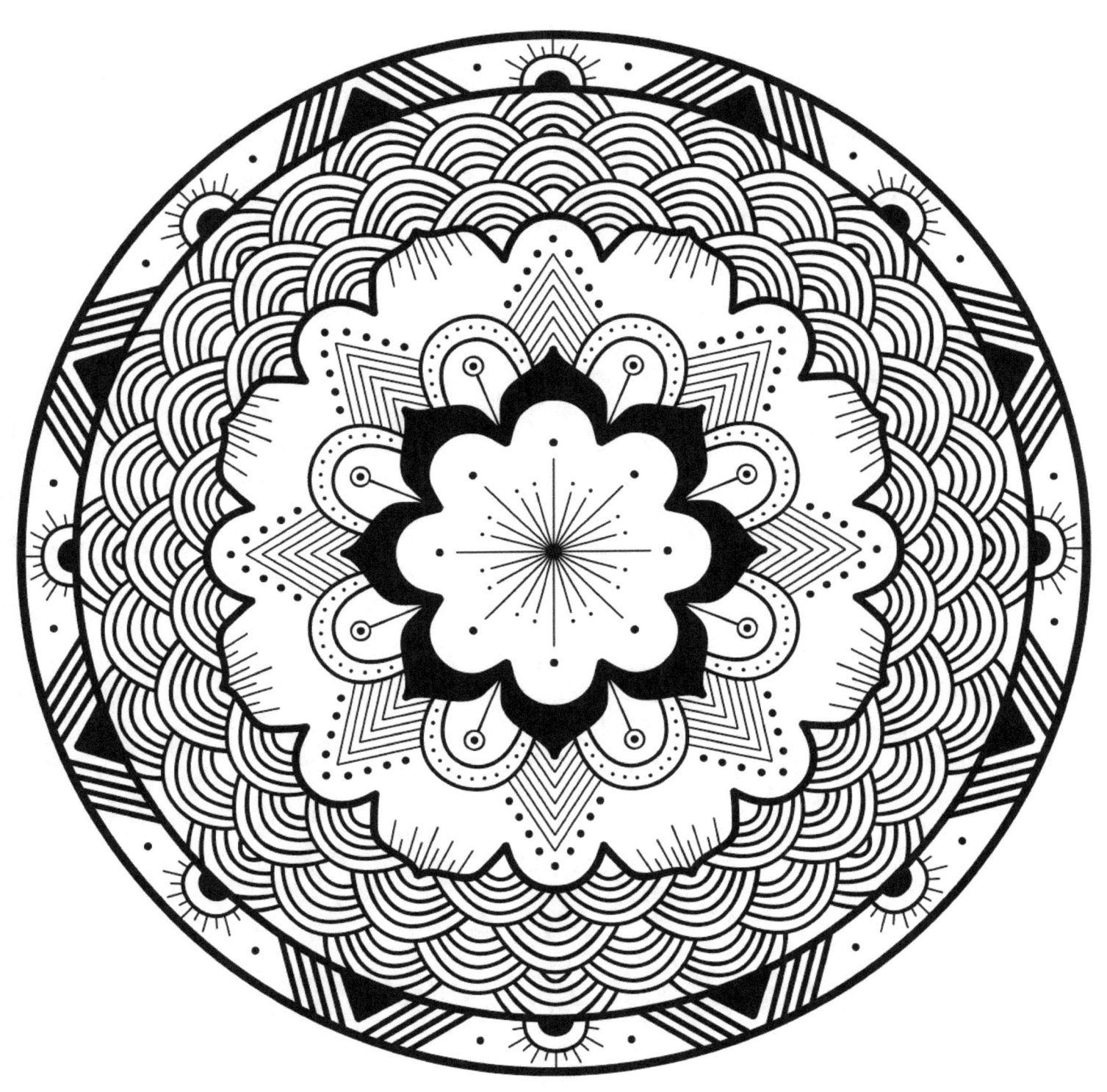

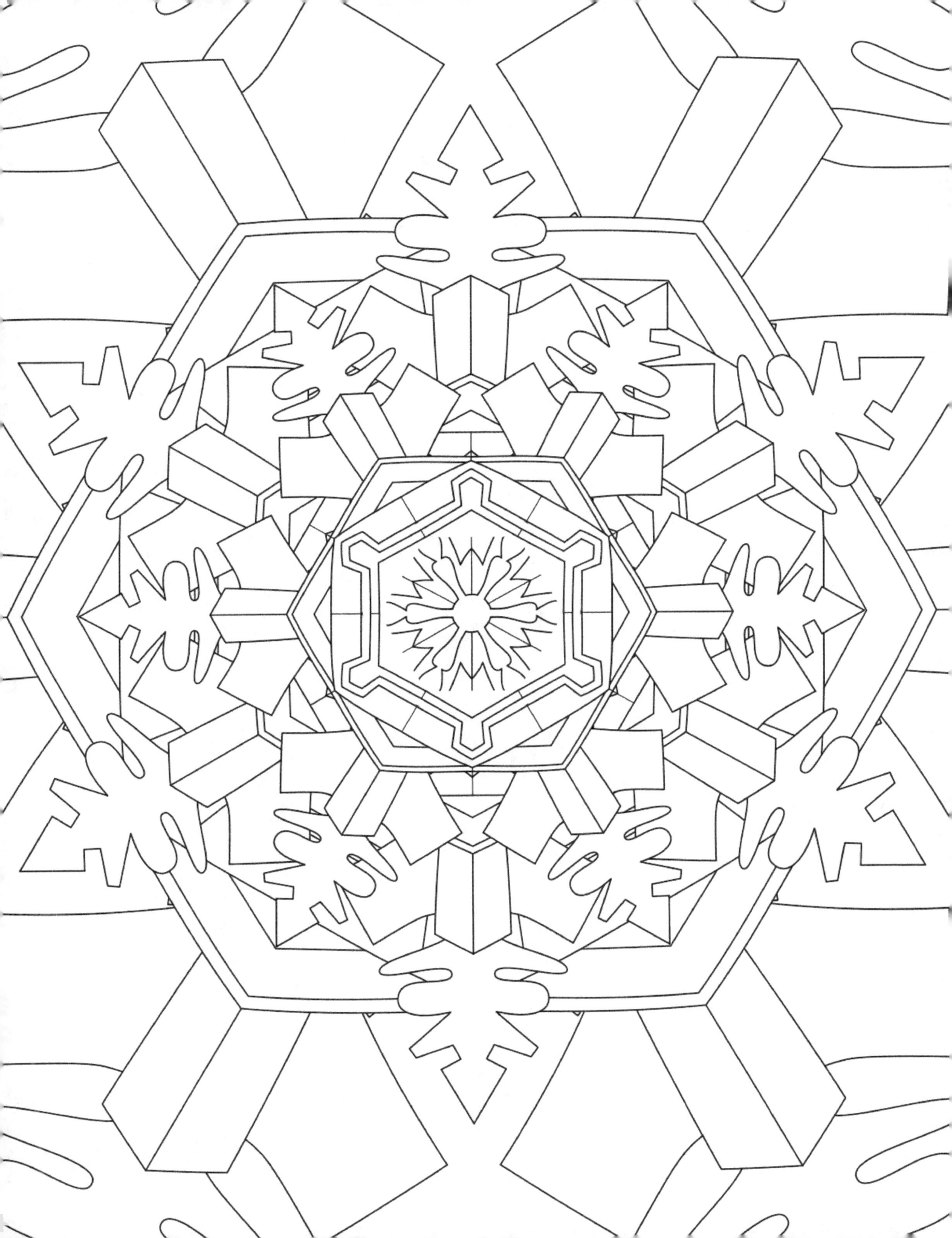

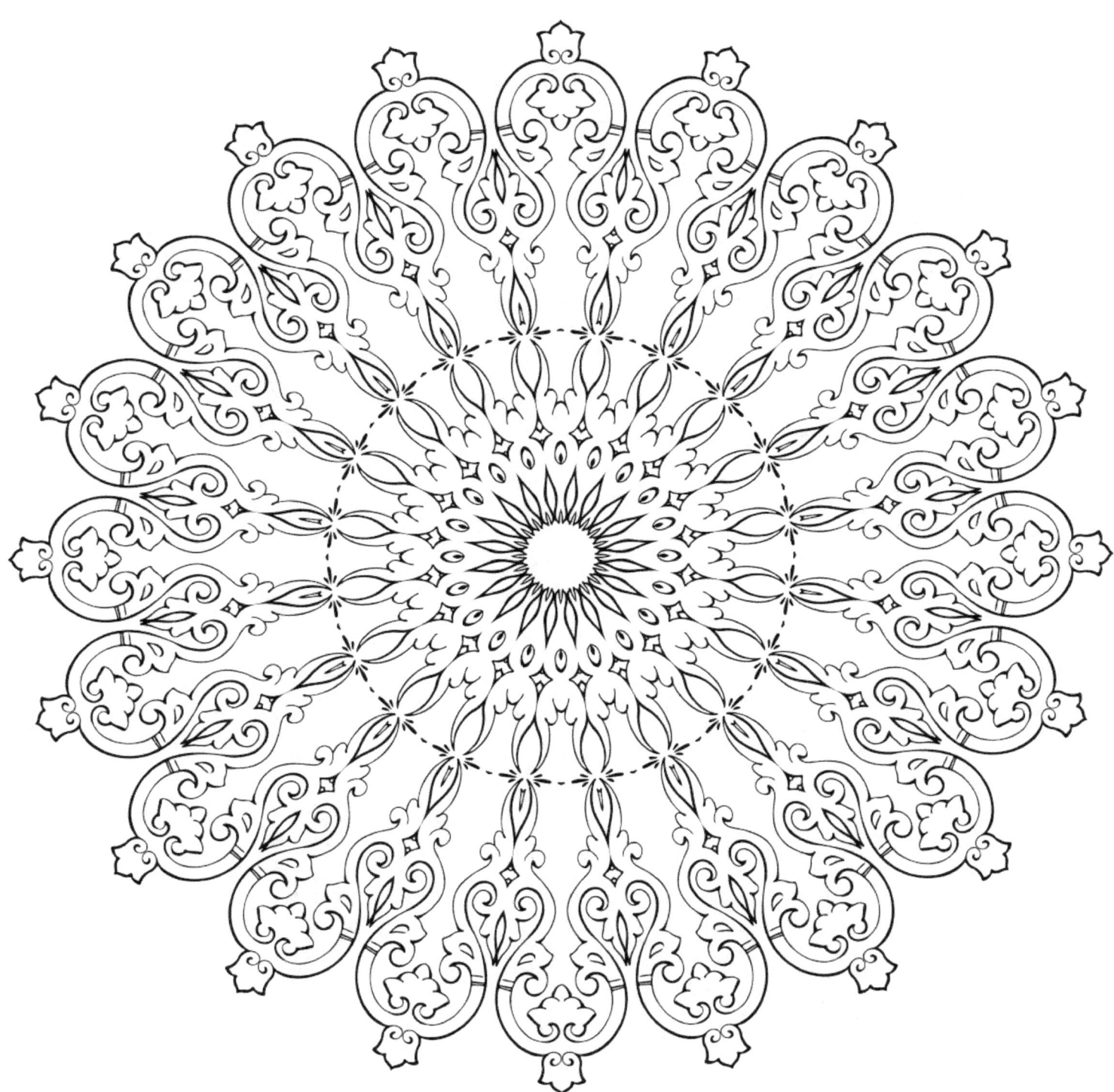

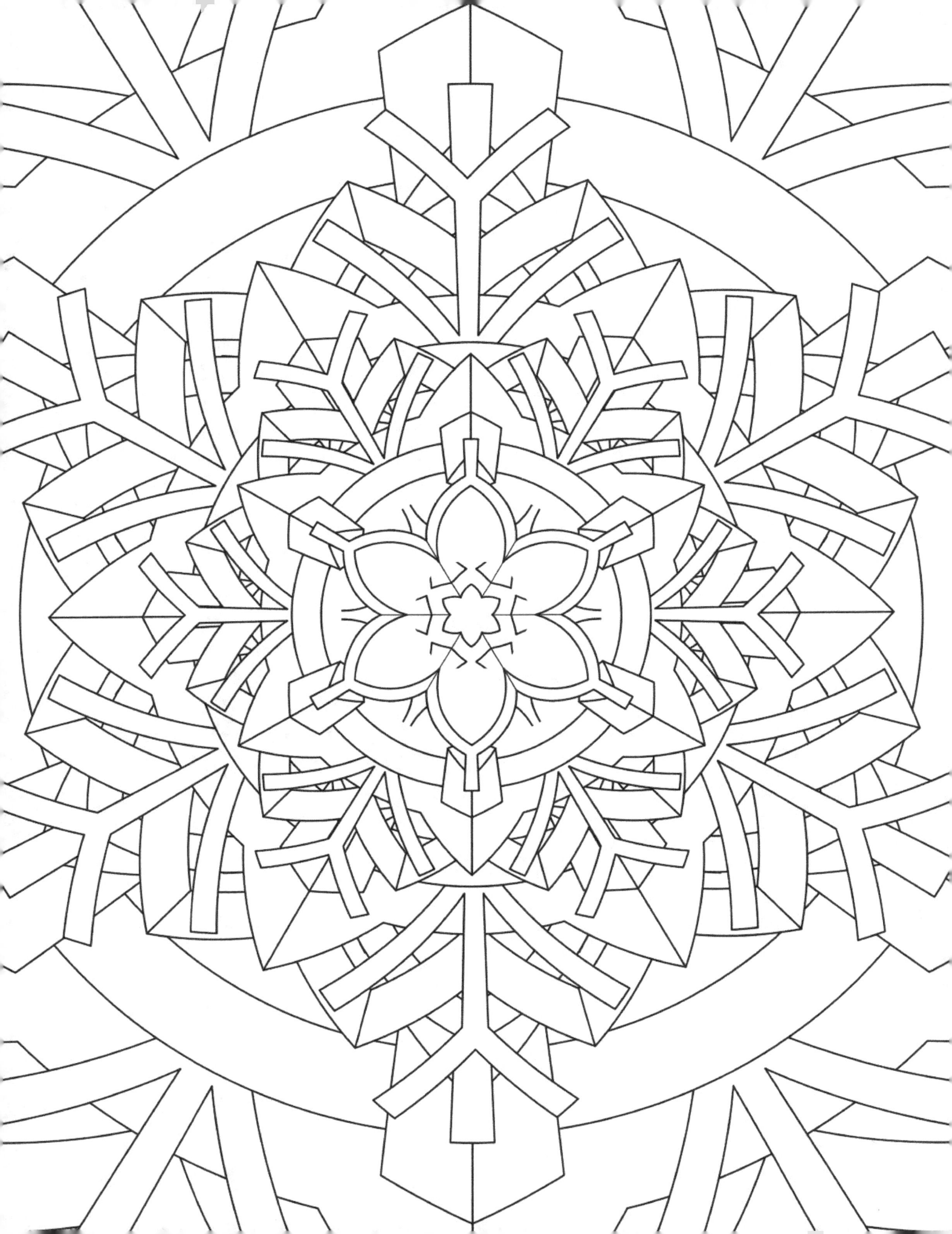

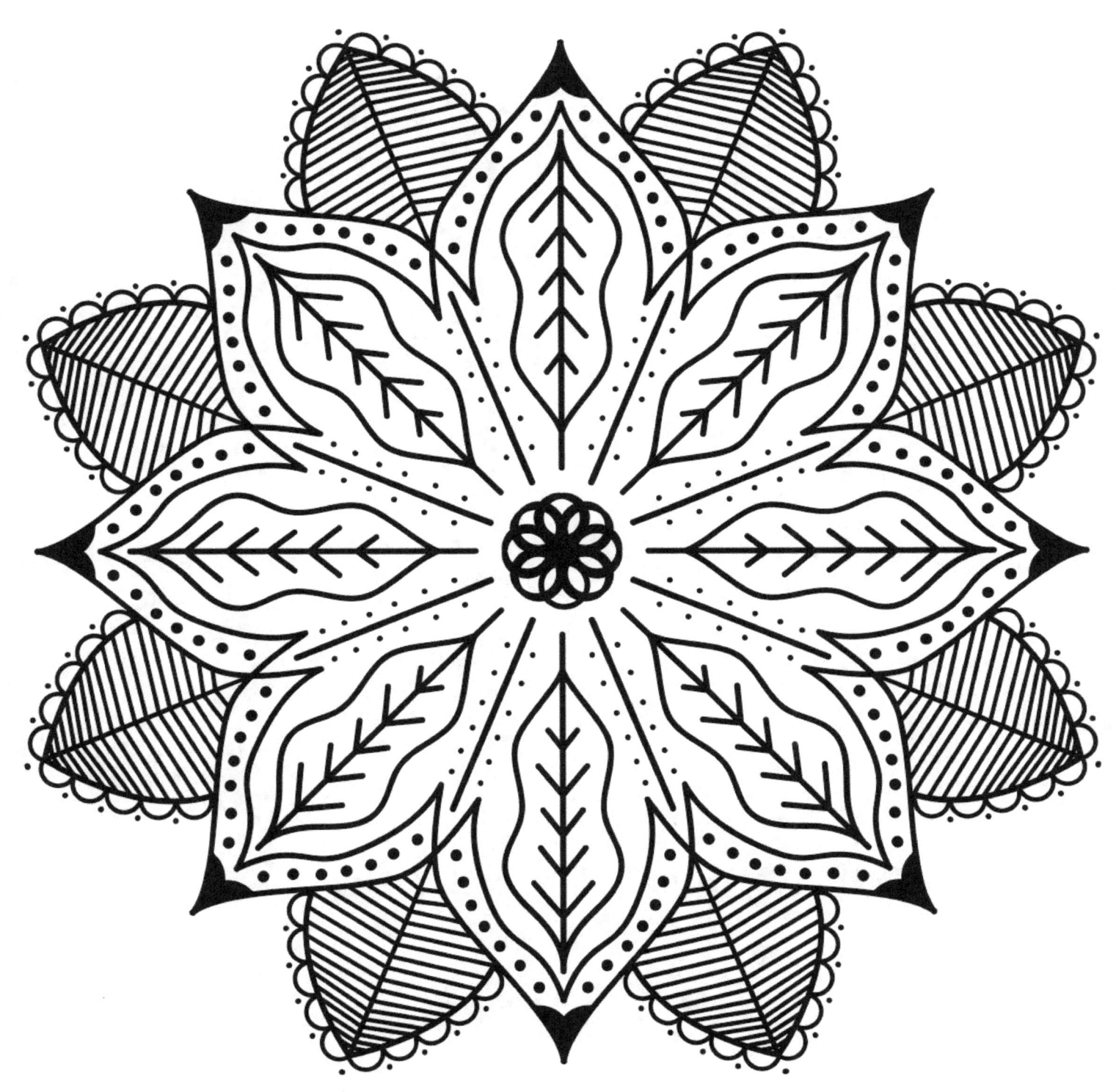

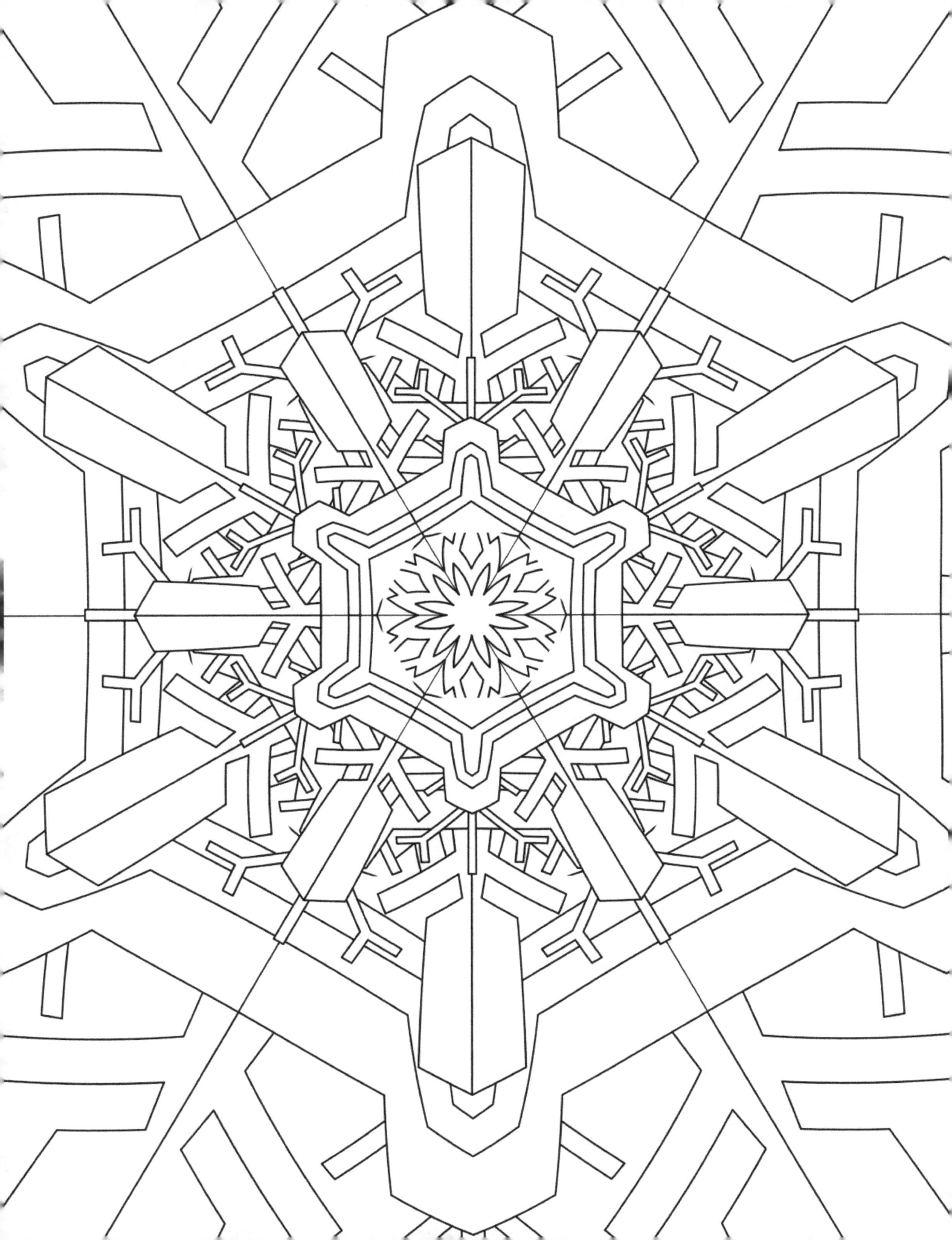

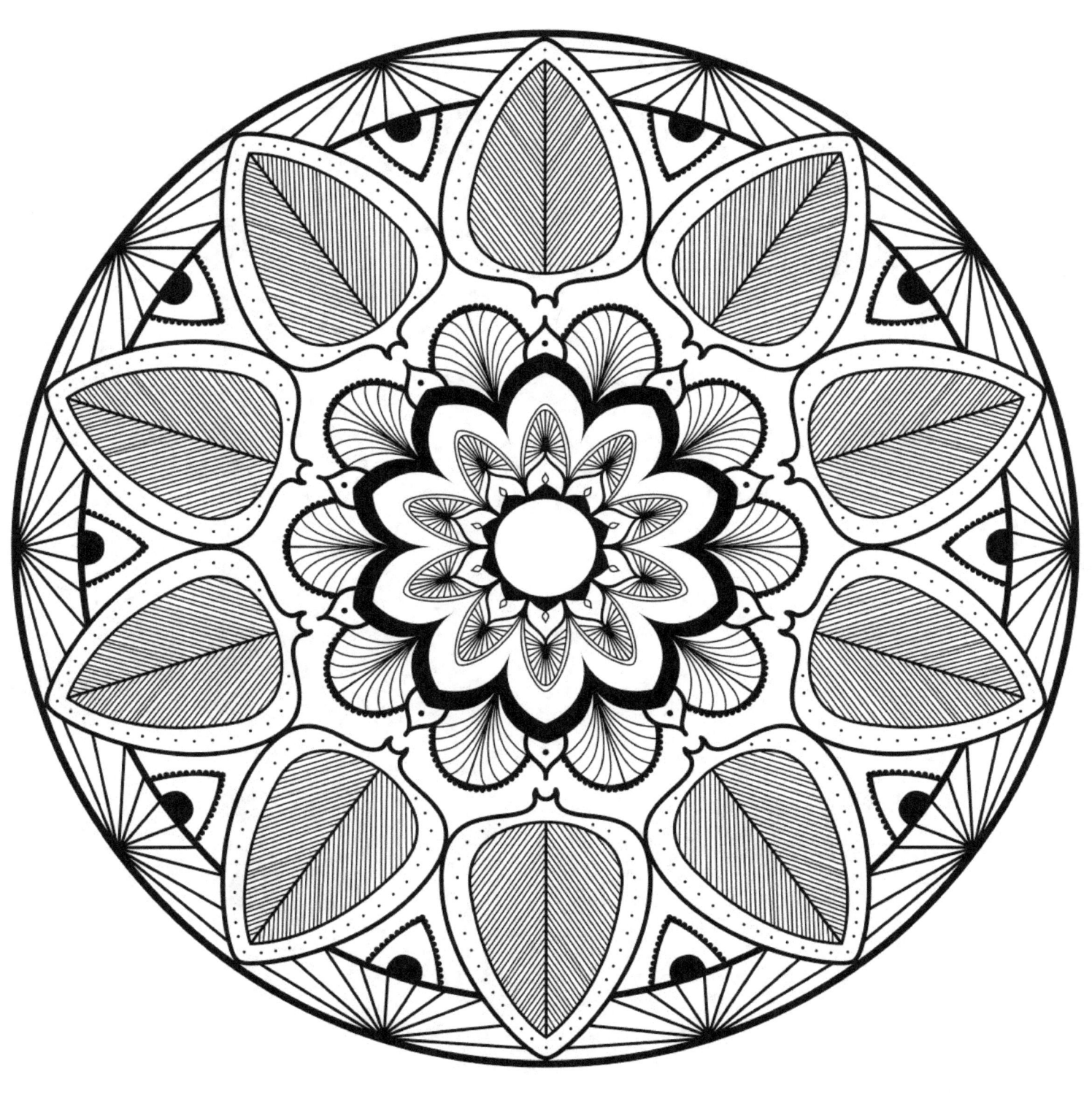

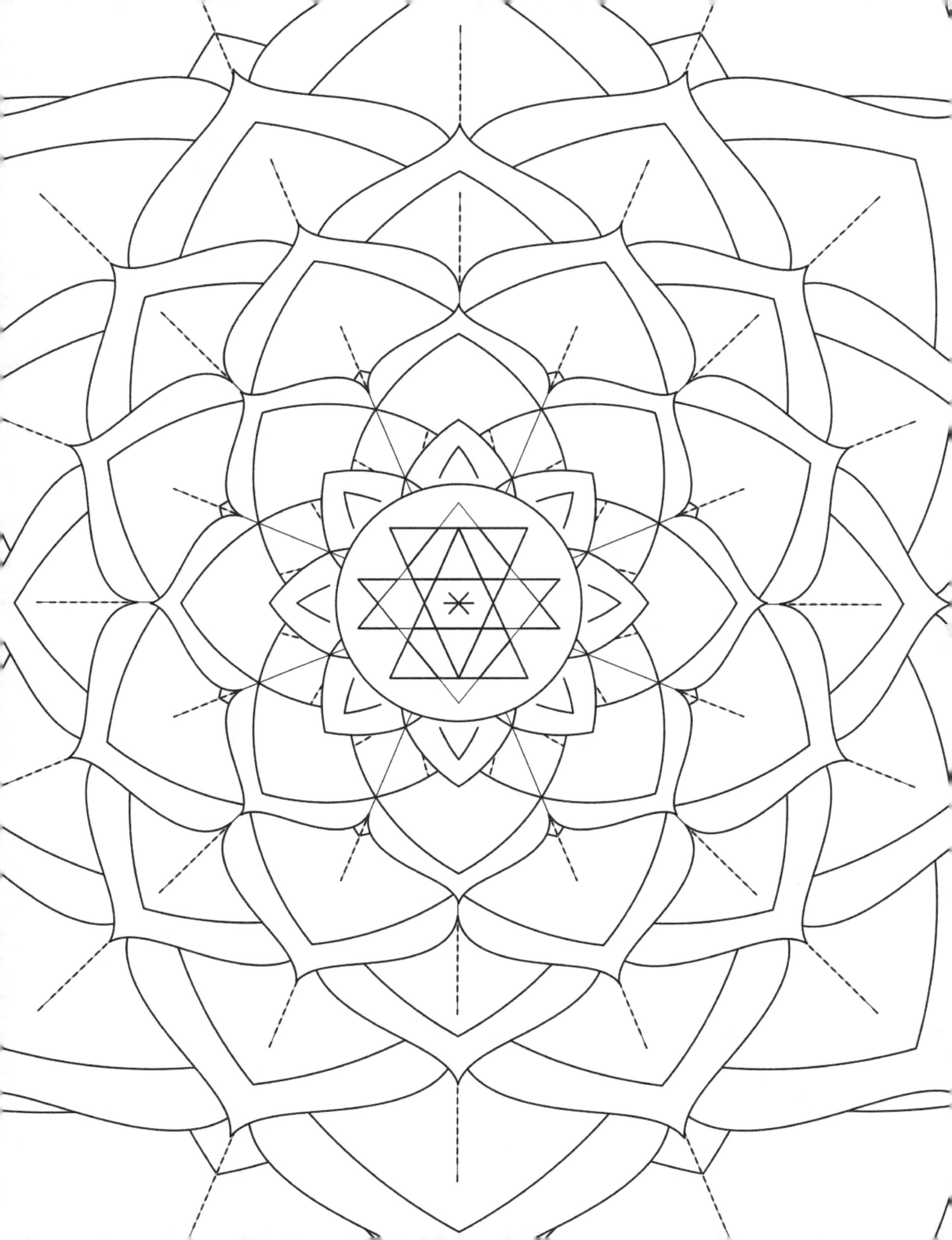

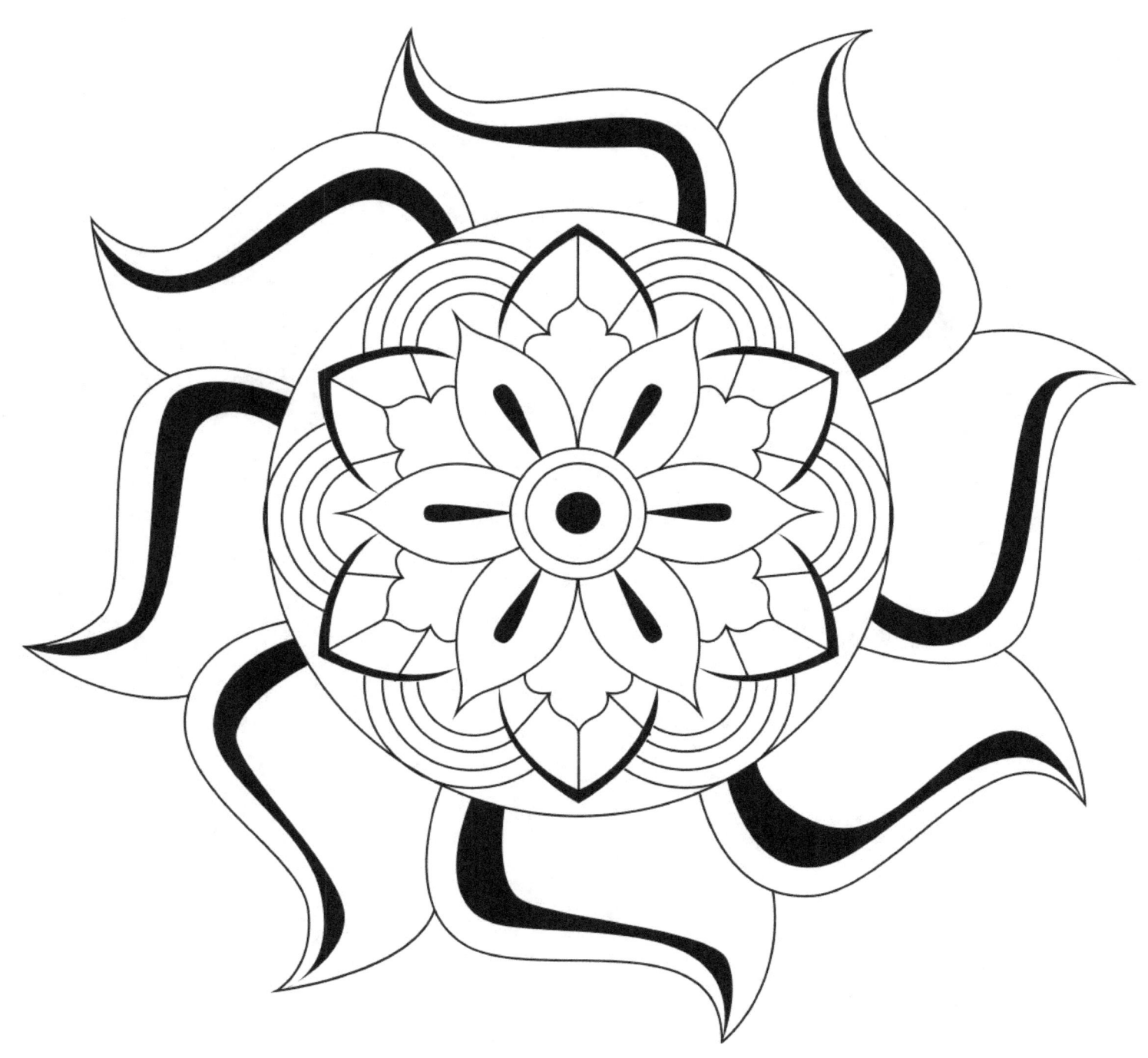

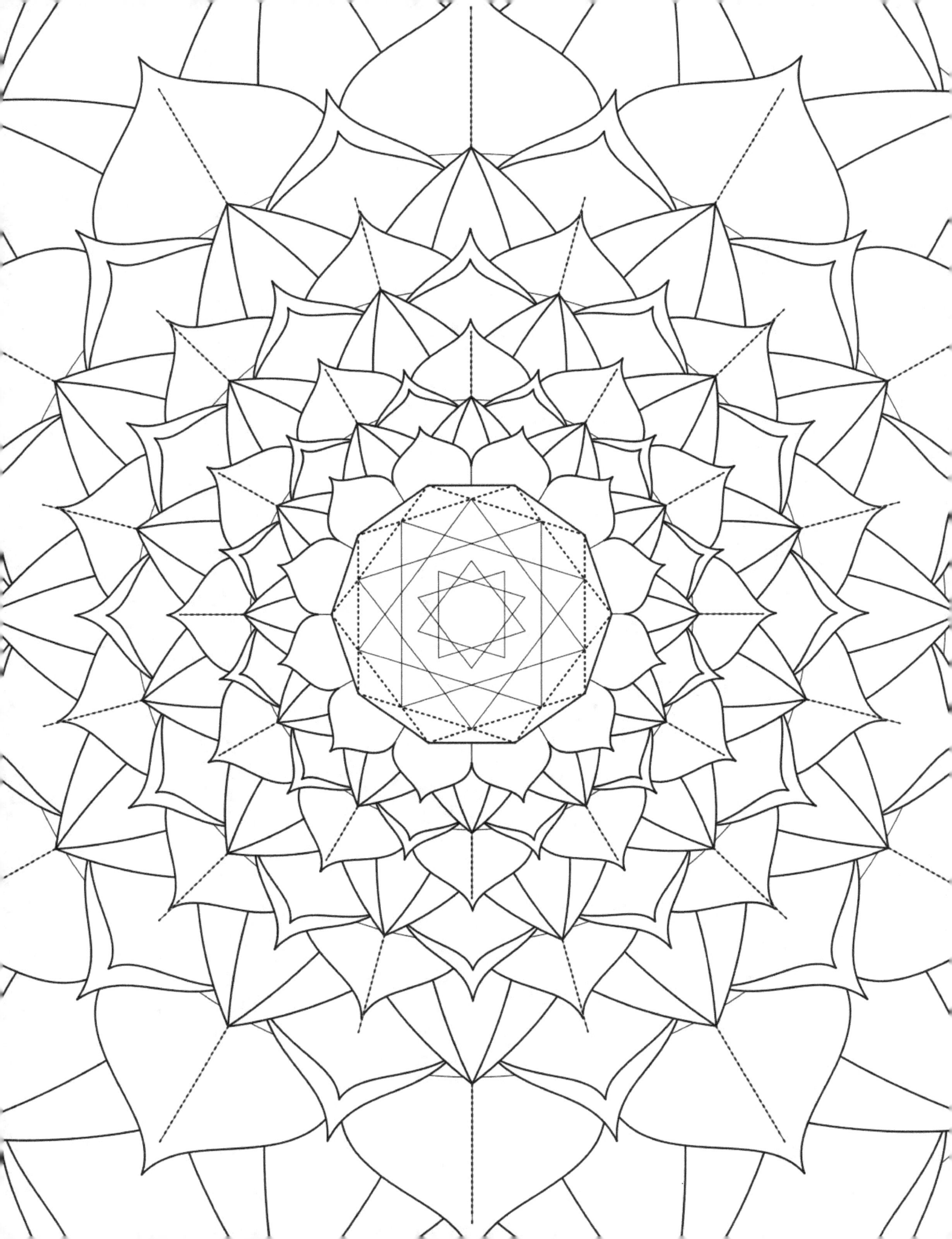

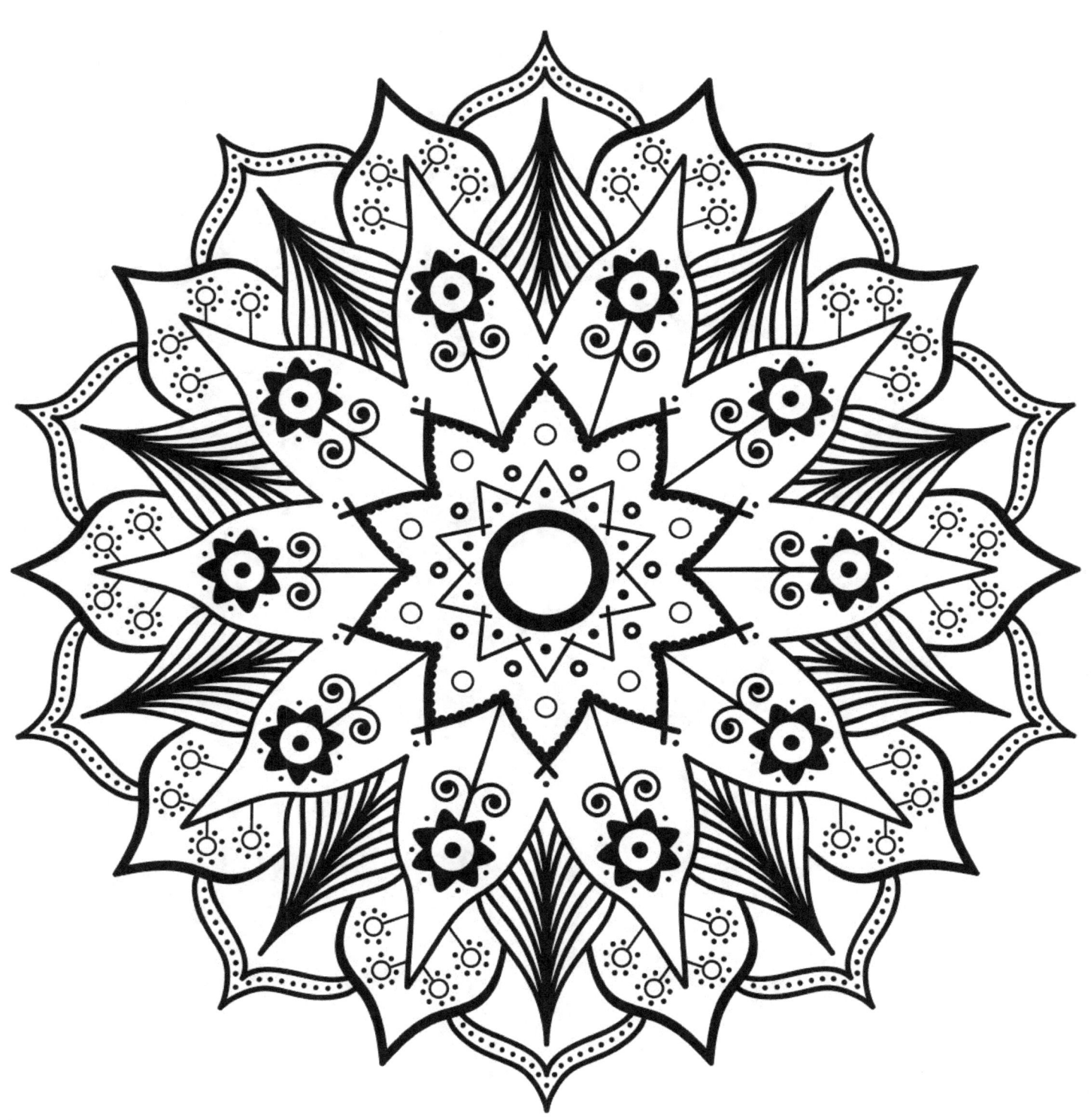

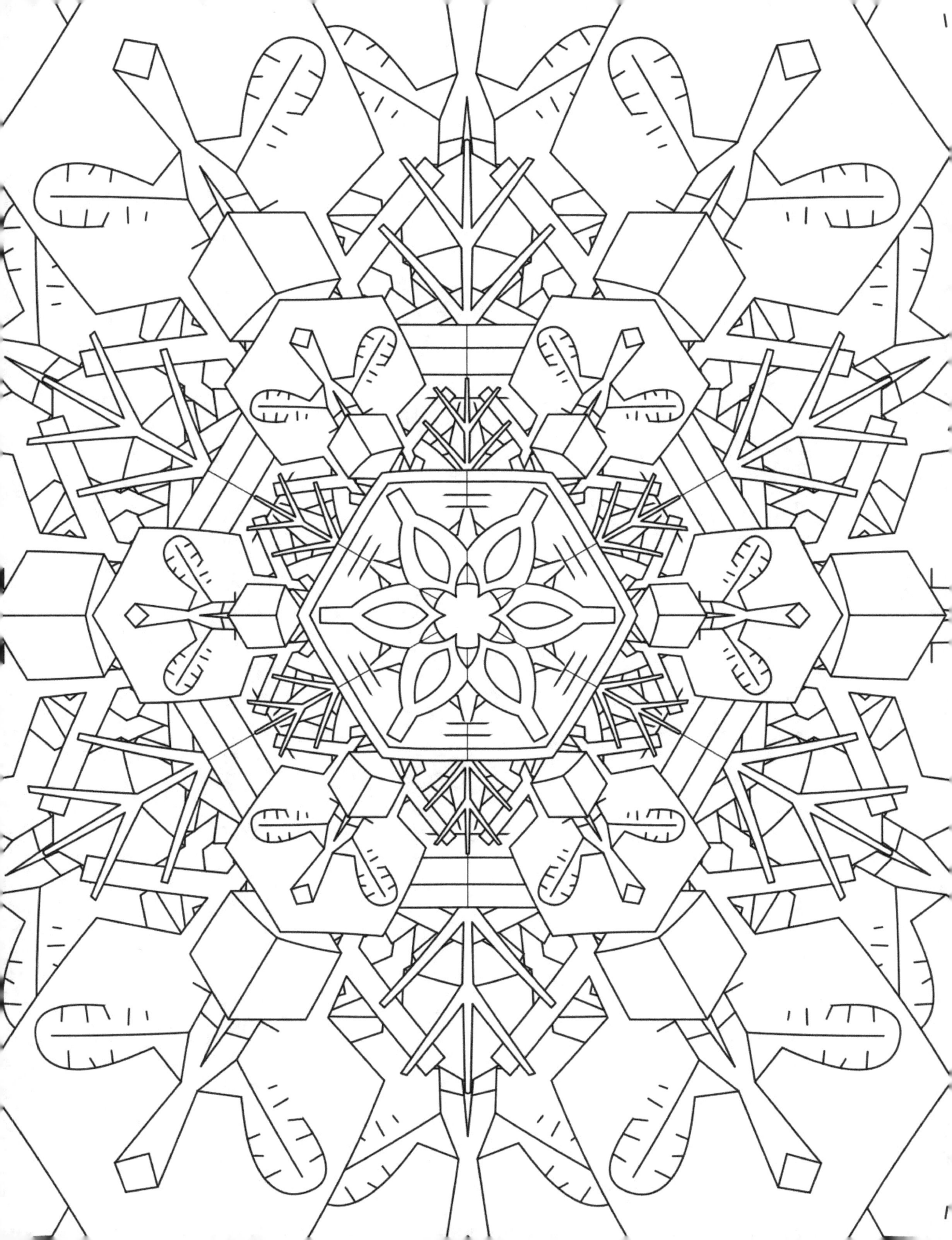

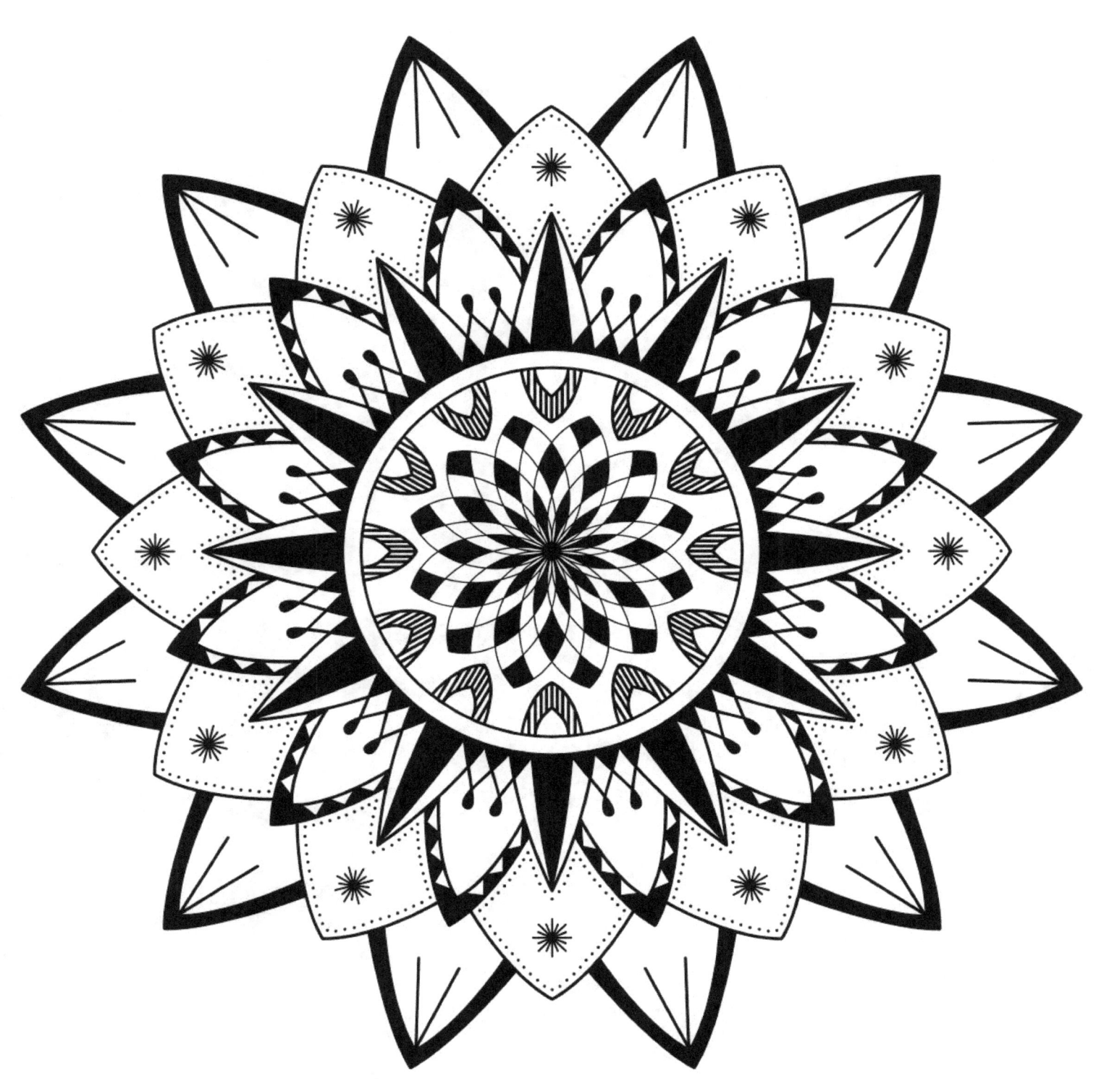

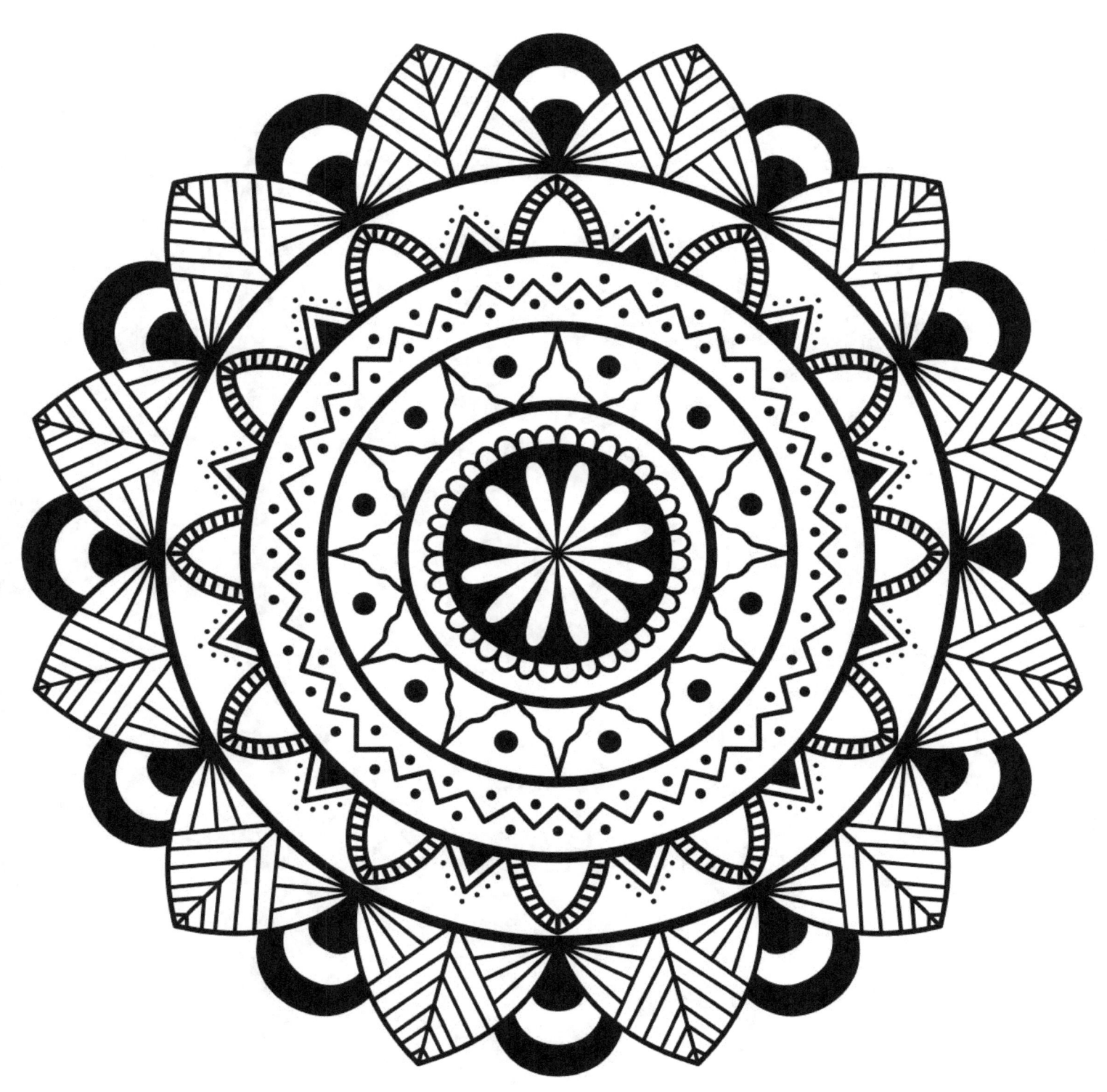

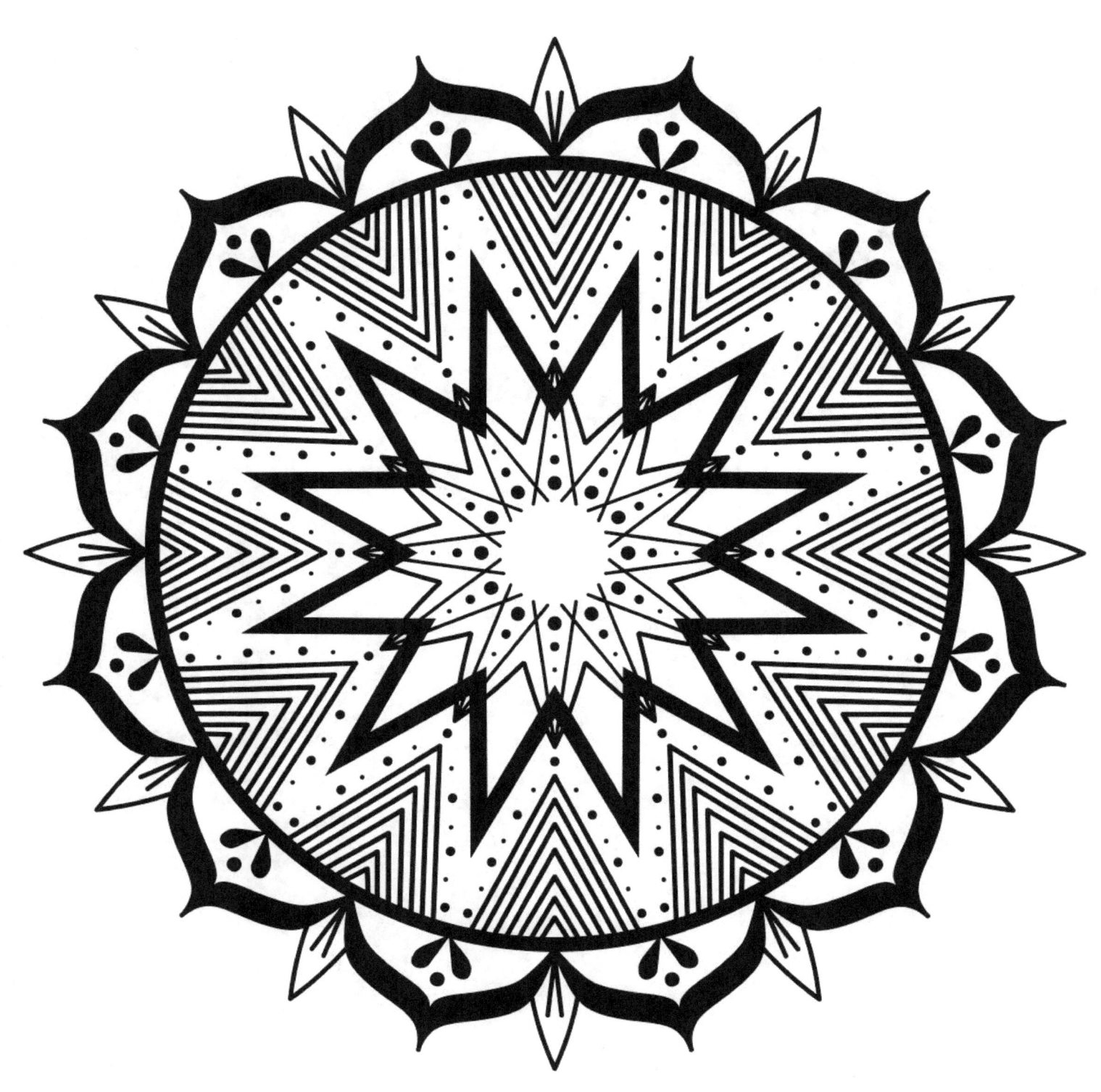

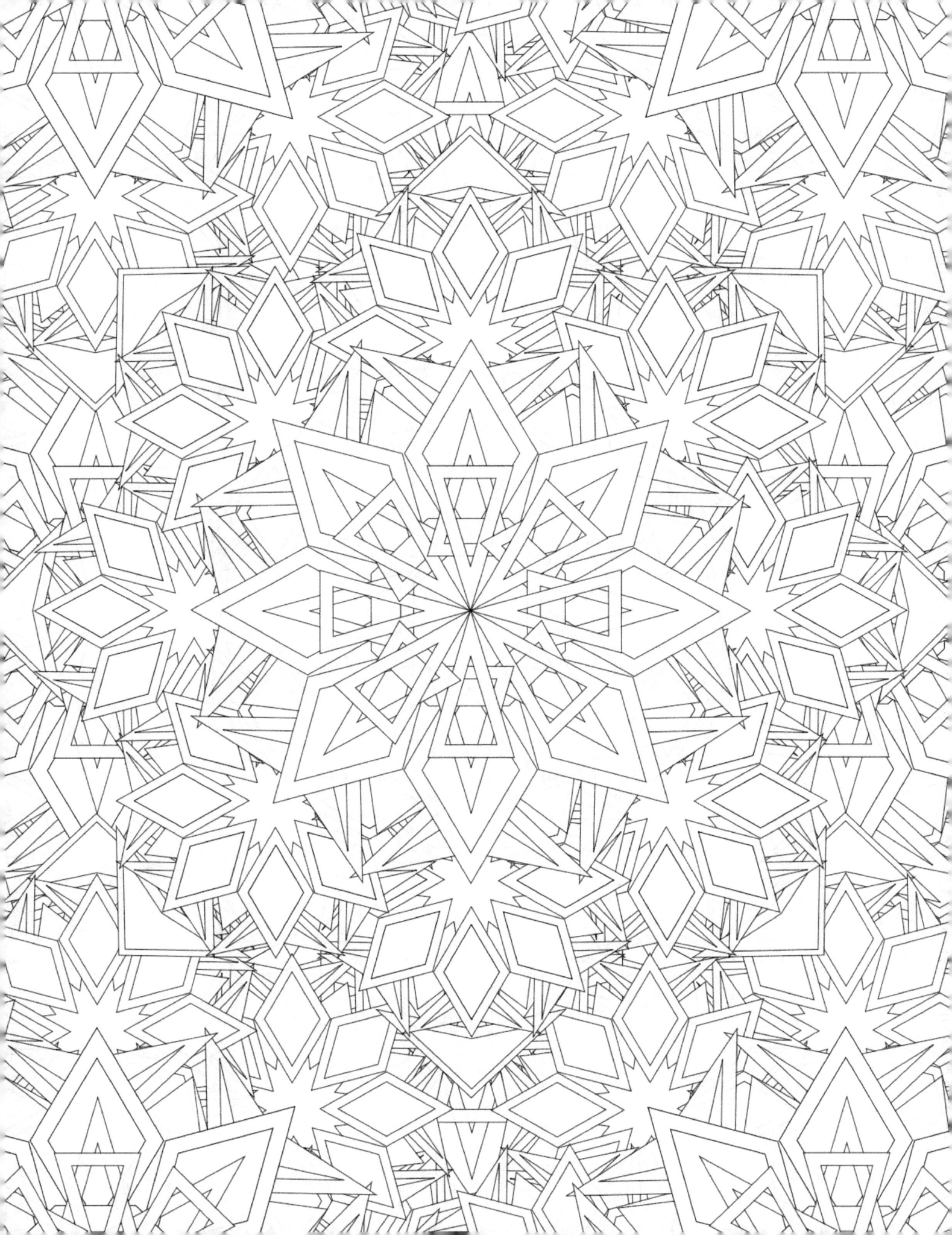

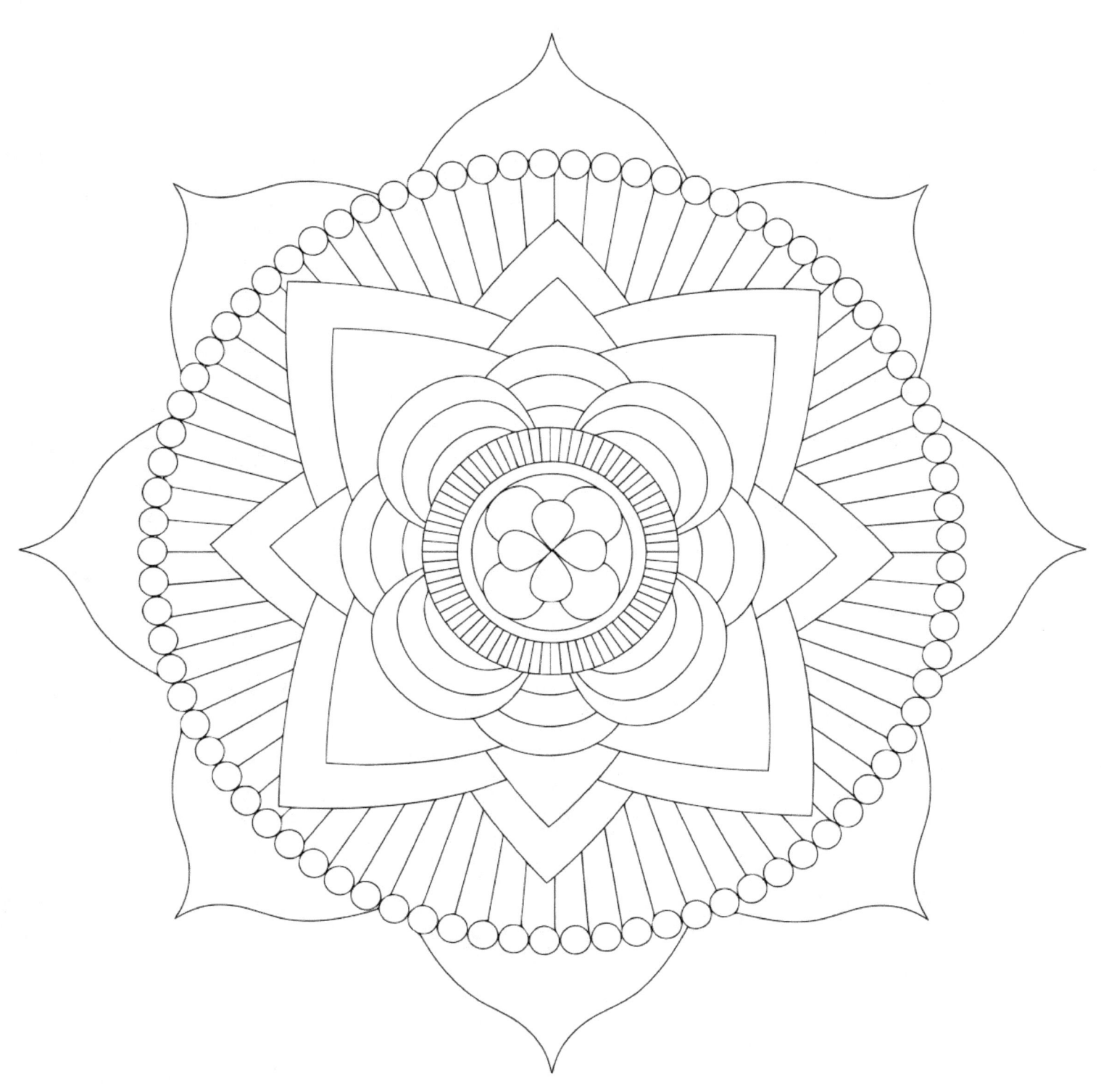

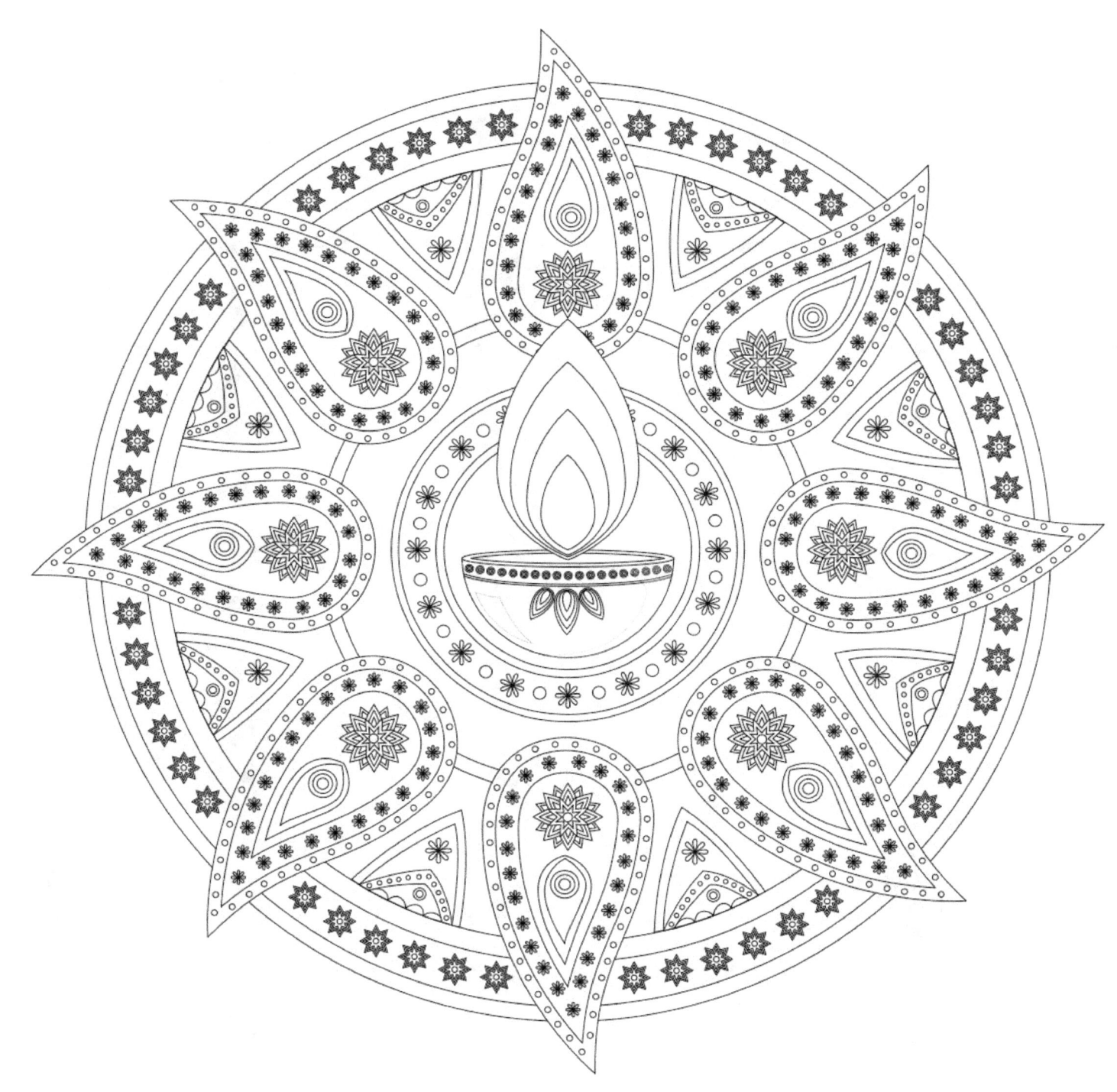

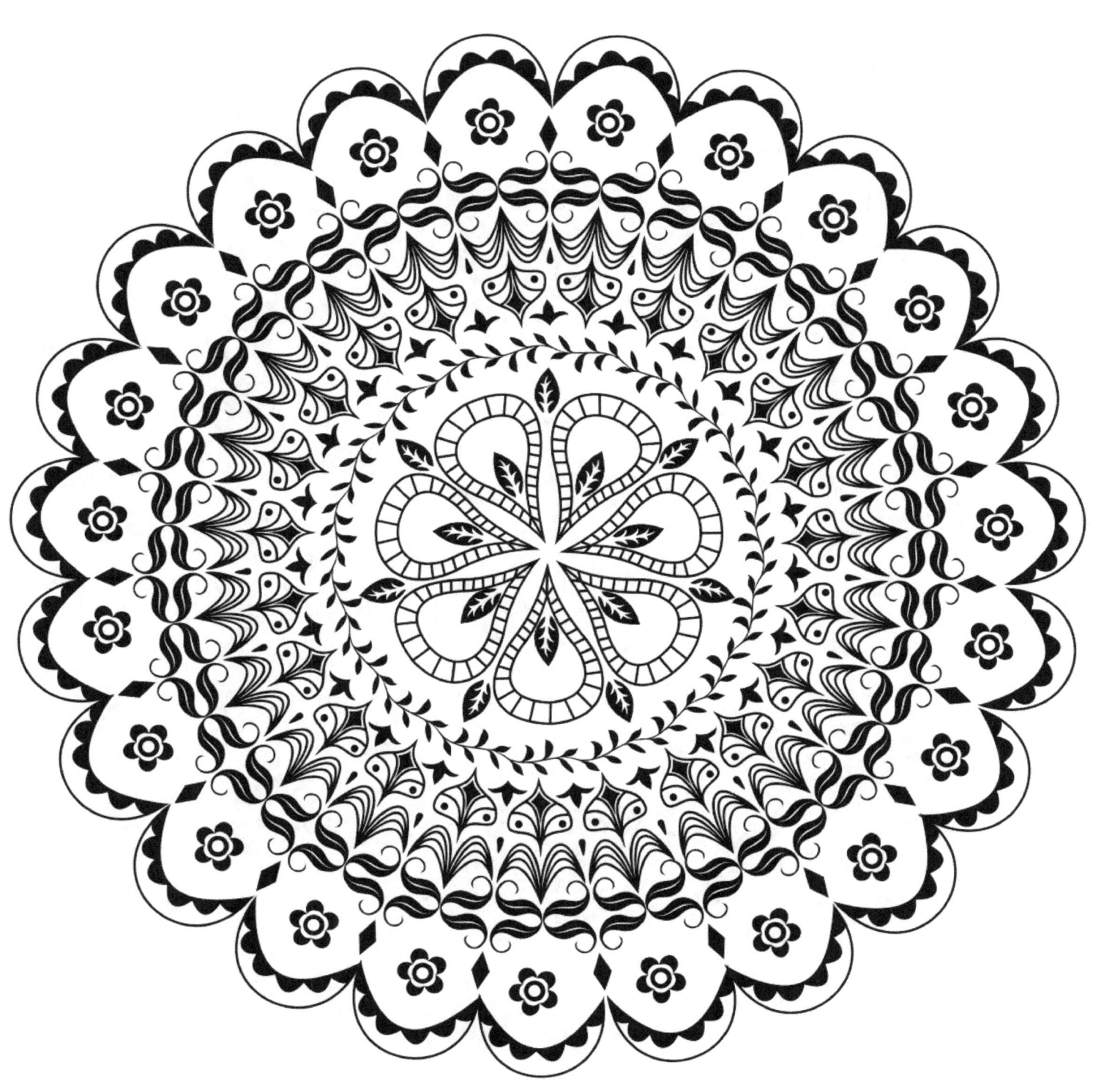

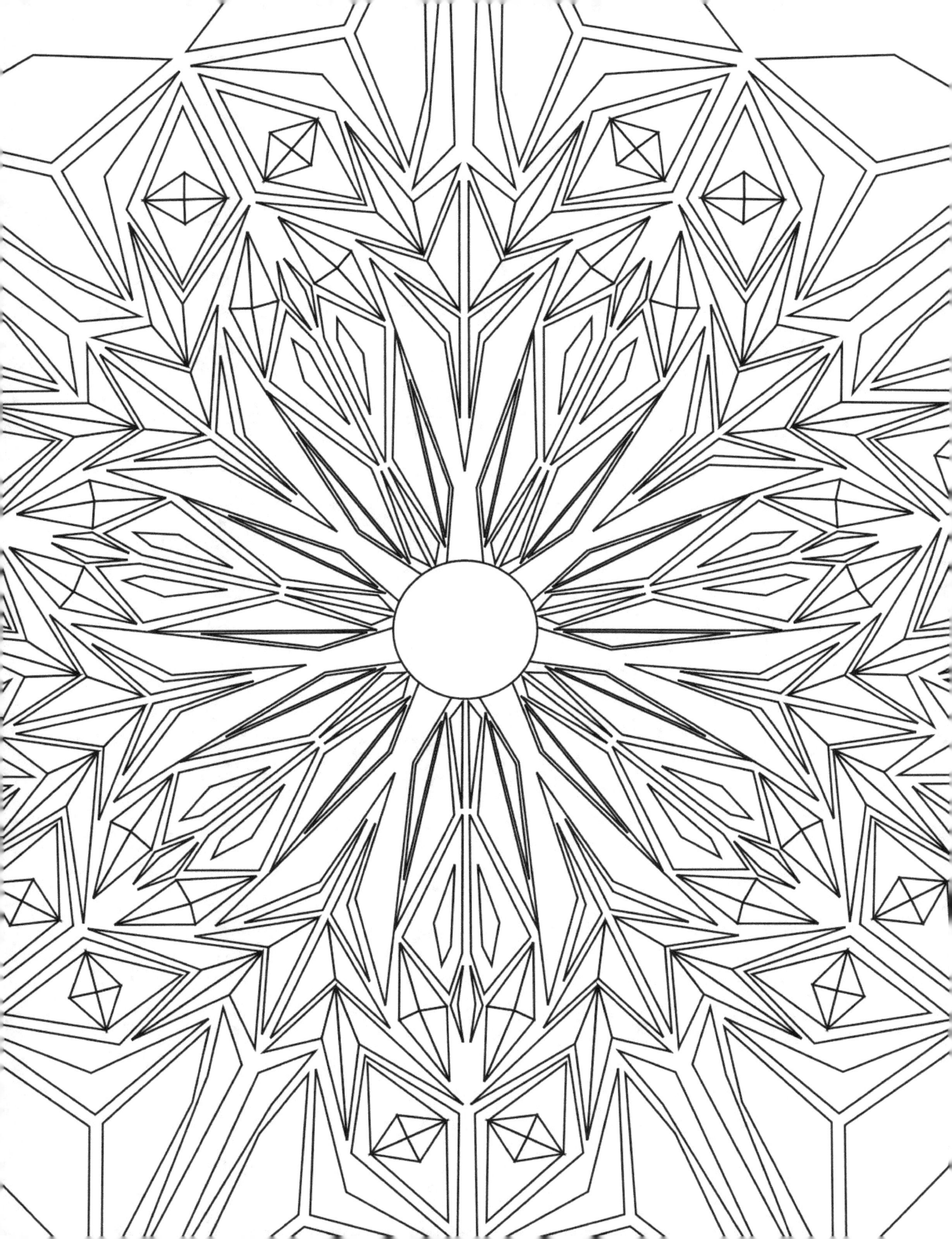

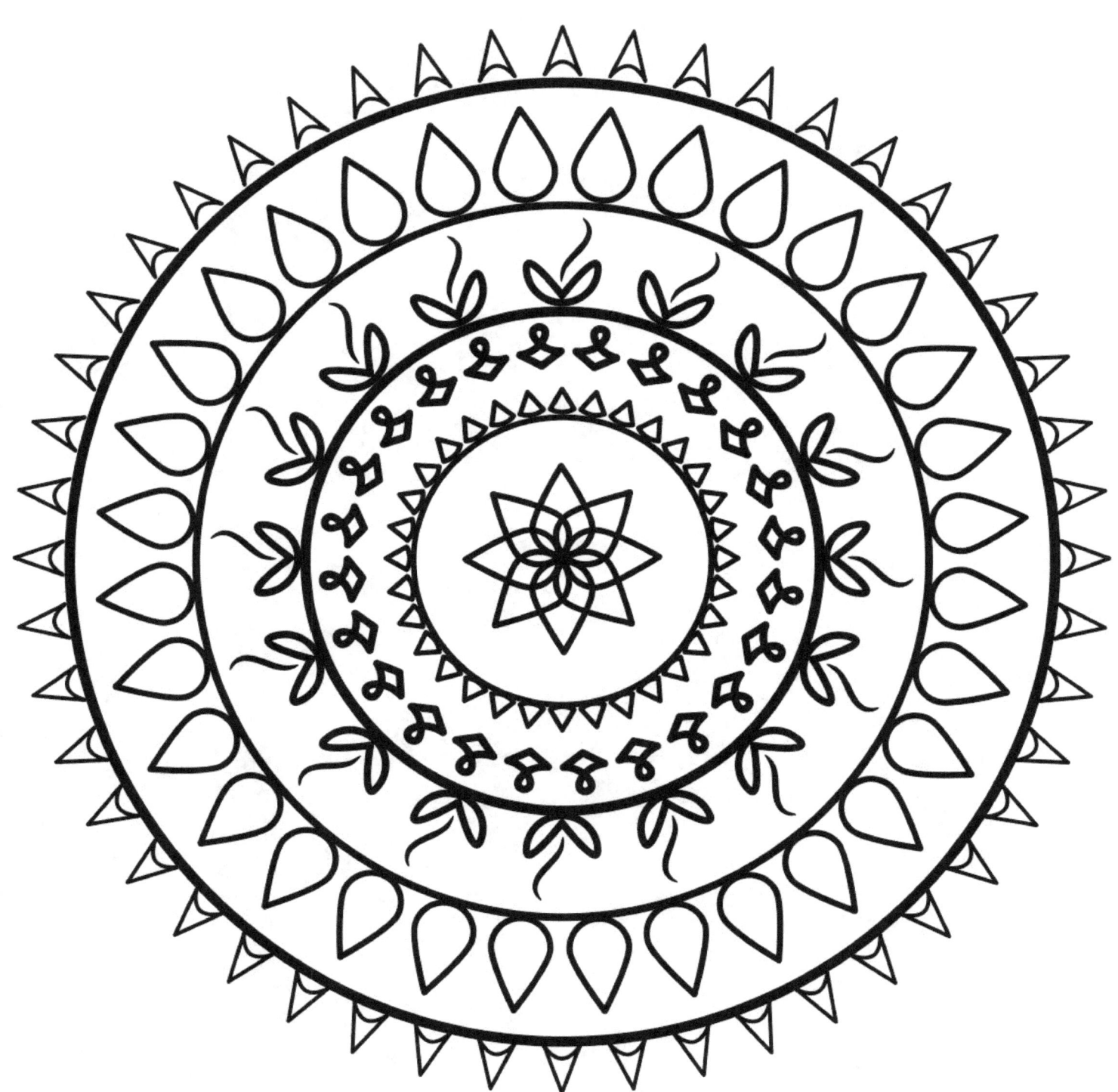

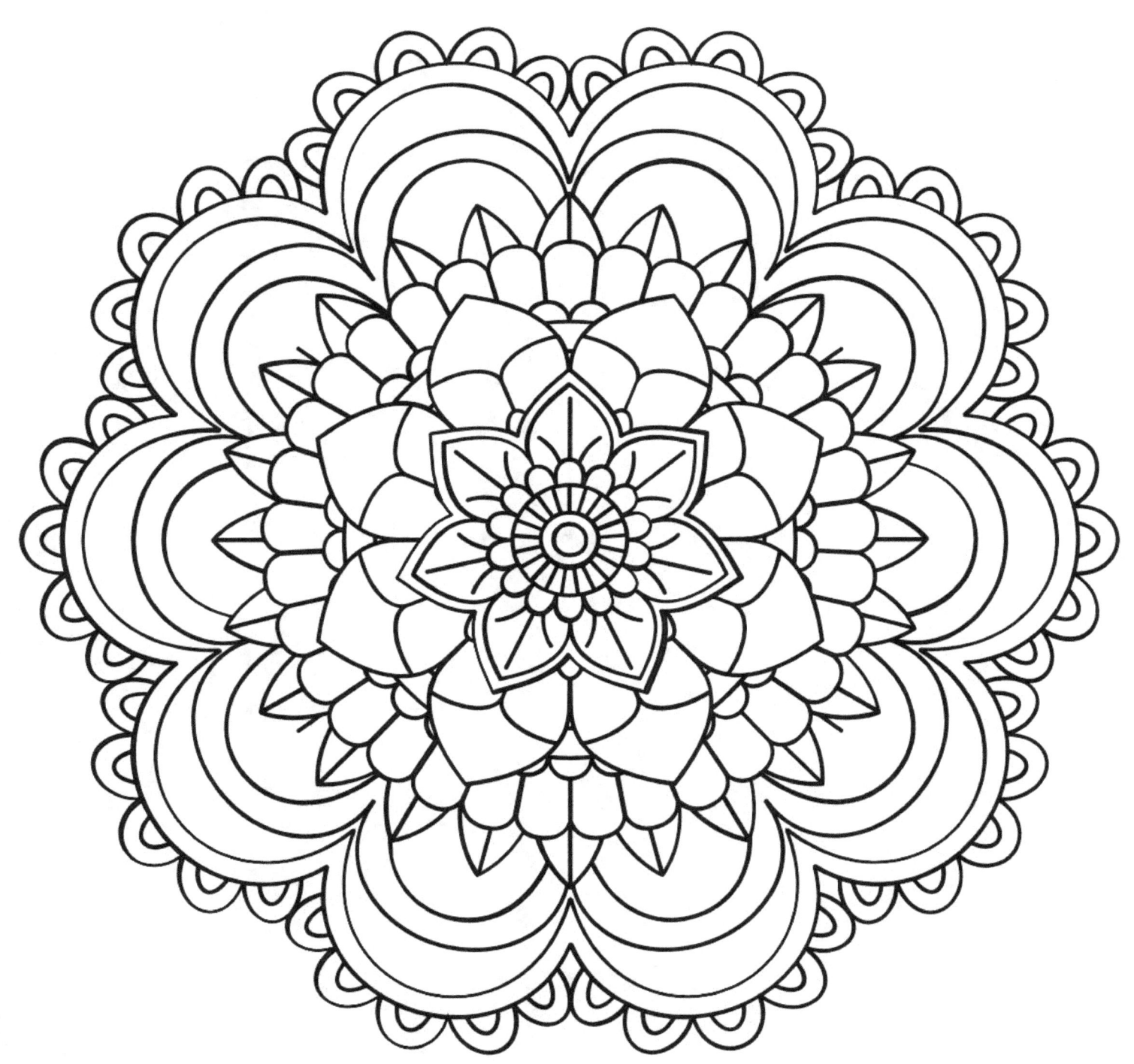

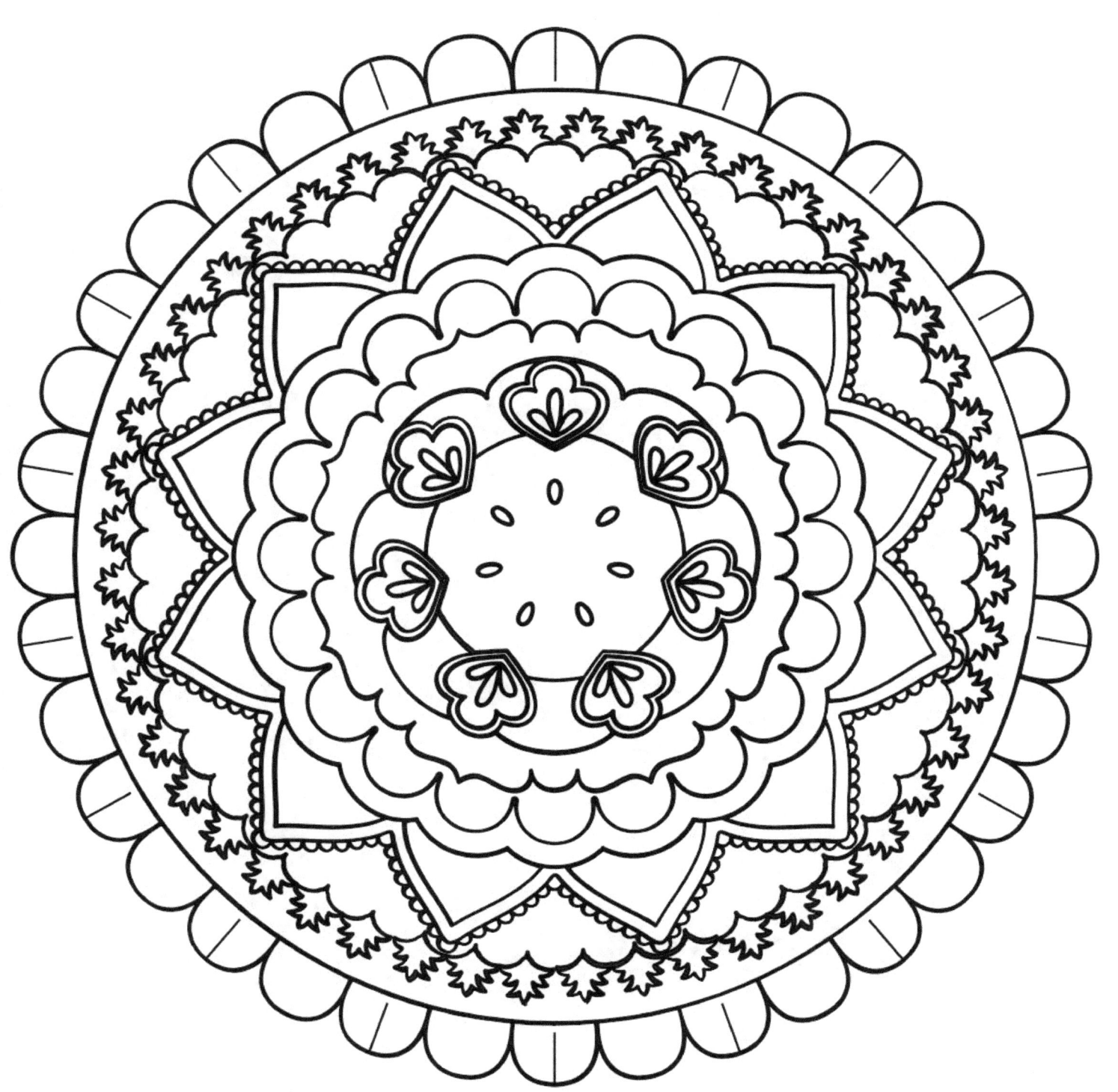

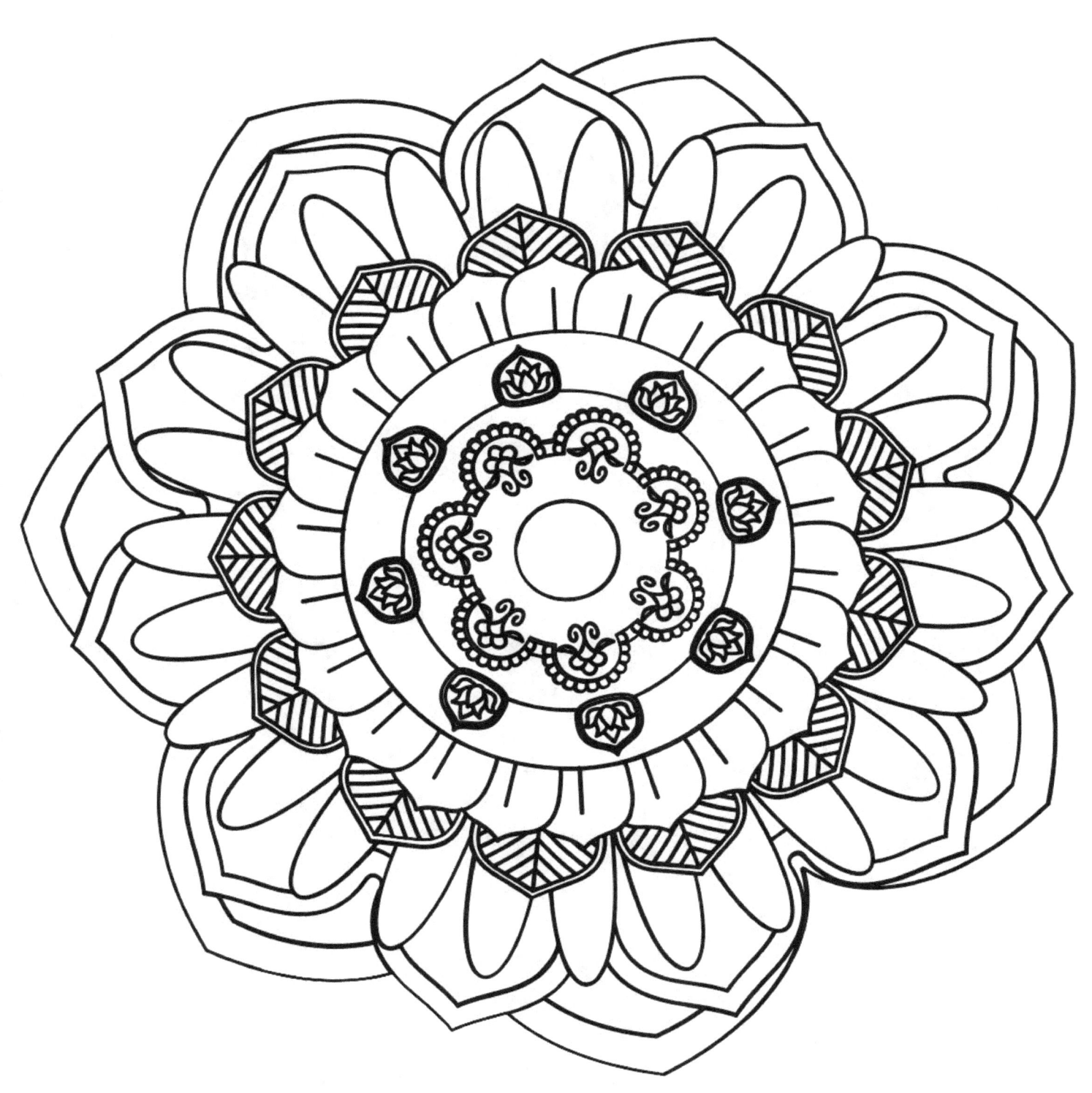

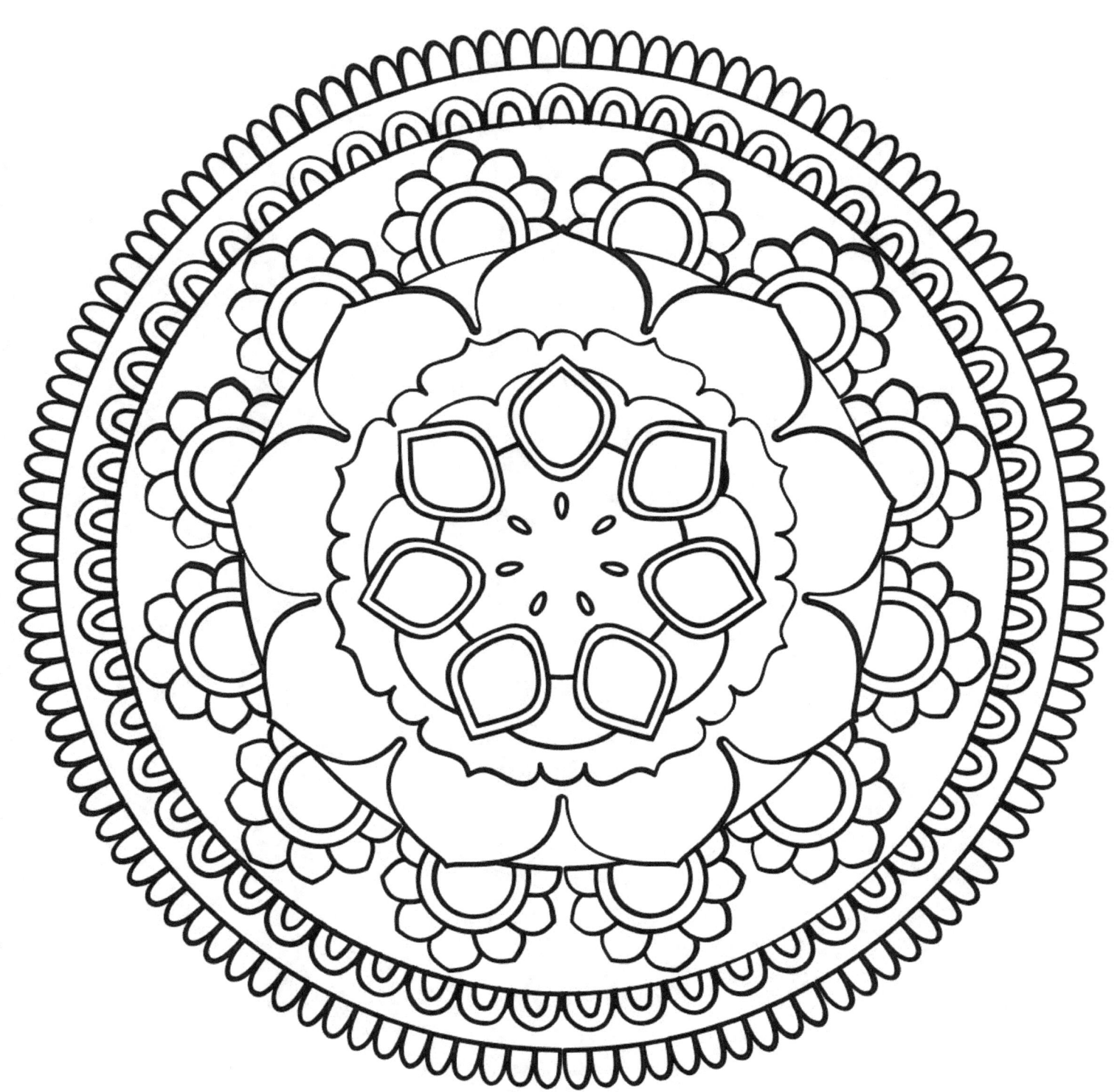

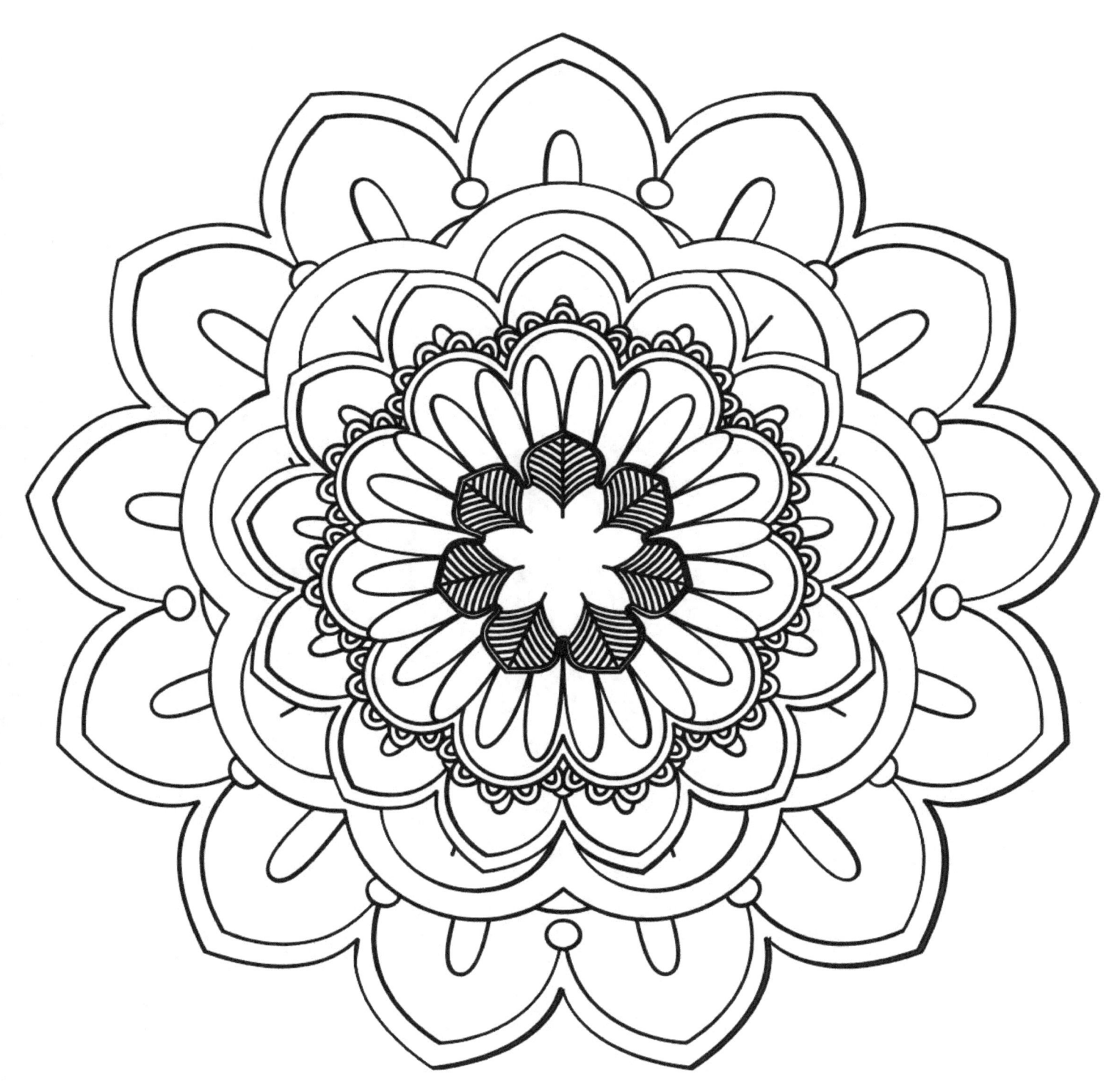

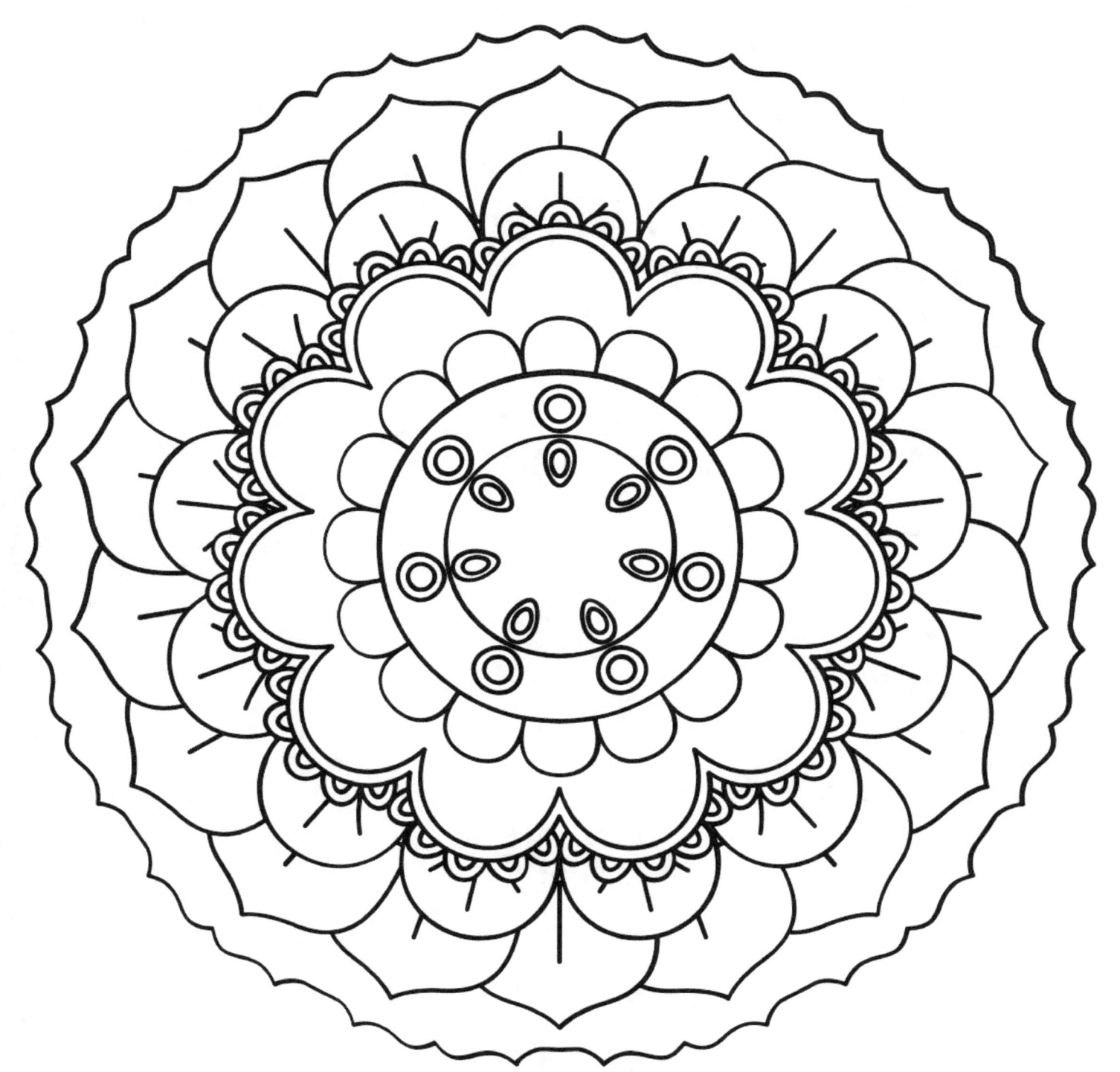

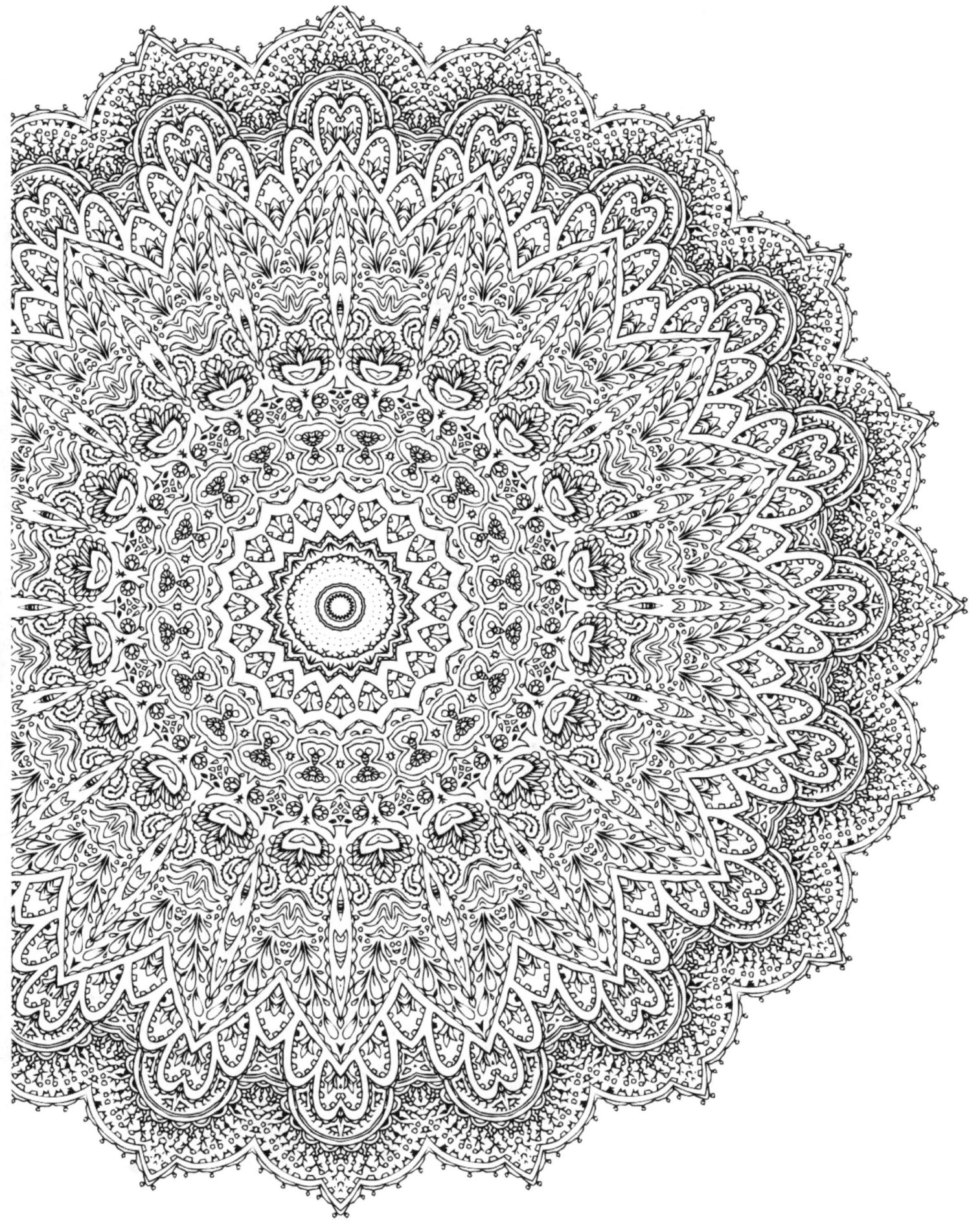

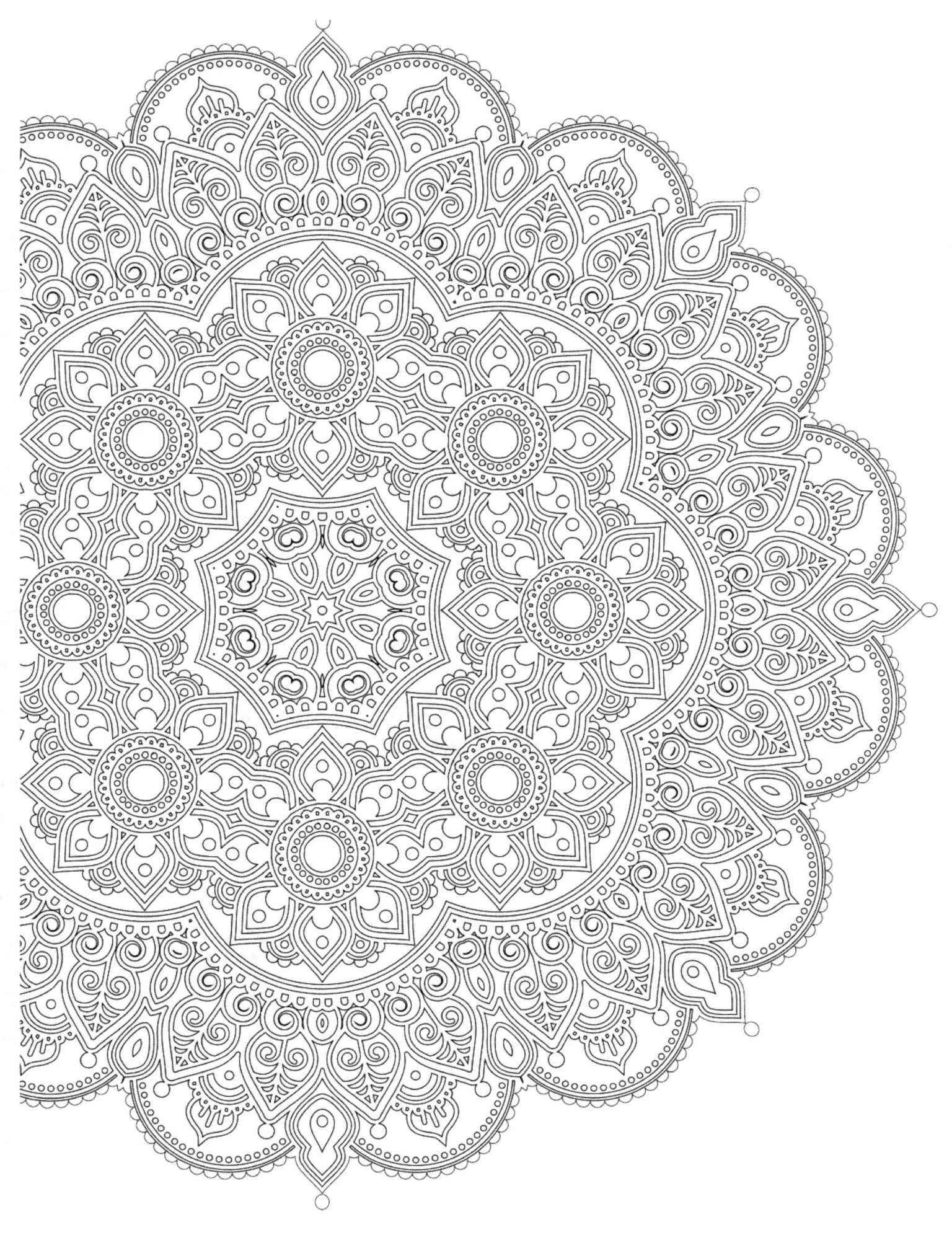

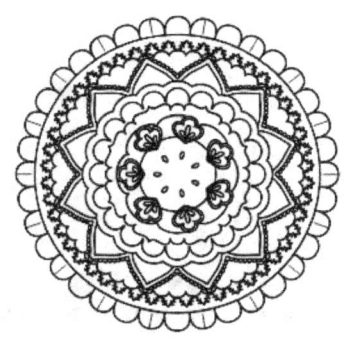

Sadly, this is the end of the Henna-style Coloring Book but hey, don't worry, you can always get another one! :)
We sincerely hope that you have enjoyed it and that it has met your expectations.
If you would like to give us any suggestions to make it better or would like to ask us a question, do not hesitate to contact us at
happyferretdesign@gmail.com
and if you would like to help us a little bit, leave a comment or rate the product at our Amazon site. That would make us even more happy! :)

You're wonderful!

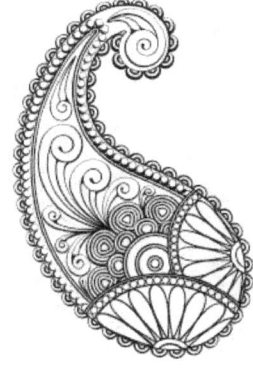

Thank you for choosing Happy Ferret Design!

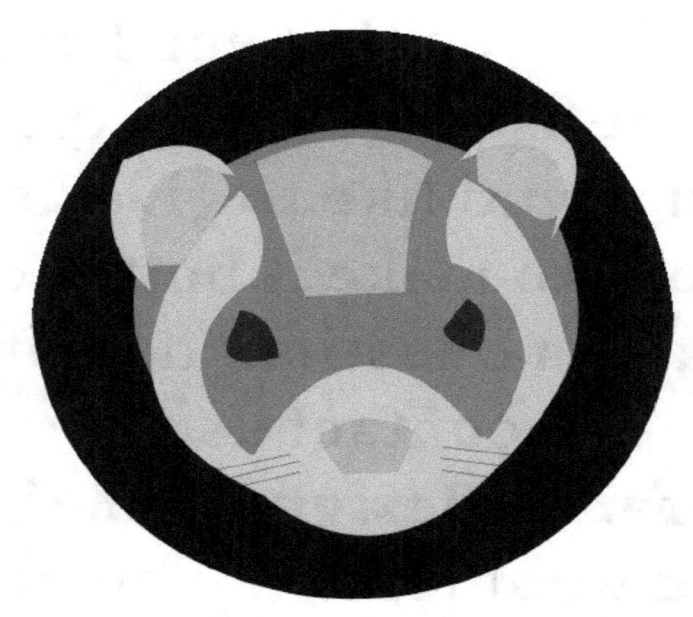

Check out our other products!